BENJAMIN FRANKLIN

AMERICAN DIPLOMACY

ITS SPIRIT AND ACHIEVEMENTS

BY

JOHN BASSETT MOORE, LL.D.

PROFESSOR OF INTERNATIONAL LAW AND DIPLOMACY
COLUMBIA UNIVERSITY

NEW YORK AND LONDON
HARPER & BROTHERS PUBLISHERS
1905

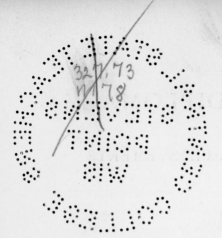

PREFATORY NOTE

In. the present volume there is reproduced, with some revision and amplification, a series of articles that appeared in *Harper's Magazine;* and one chapter—the fourth—has been added. The primary object of the work is to give, not a chronological narrative of international transactions, but rather an exposition of the principles by which they were guided, in order that the distinctive purposes of American diplomacy may be understood and its meaning and influence appreciated. Nothing could be more erroneous than the supposition that the United States has, as the result of certain changes in its habits, suddenly become, within the past few years, a "world-power." The United States has in reality always been, in the fullest and highest sense, a world-power; and the record of its achievements in the promulgation and spread of liberal and humane doctrines is one in which no American need hesitate to own a patriotic pride.

J. B. M.

CONTENTS

ILLUSTRATIONS

THE CONDUCT OF FOREIGN IN-
TERCOURSE

PRIOR to the adoption of the Constitution, the
executive as well as the legislative power of the
United States resided in the Congress. For the
purpose of conducting foreign intercourse, the Continental Congress established on November 29, 1775,
a Committee of Secret Correspondence. This committee was superseded on April 17, 1777, by the
Committee for Foreign Affairs. The committee
plan having proved to be utterly inefficient, there
was created on January 10, 1871, the Department of
Foreign Affairs, to be presided over by a Secretary of
Foreign Affairs. The first person to fill this office
was Robert R. Livingston, who was elected August
10, 1781. He entered upon his duties October 20,
1781, and served till June 4, 1783. His successor
was John Jay, who assumed charge of the office on
September 21, 1784. By the act of July 27, 1789,
under the Constitution, the Department of Foreign
Affairs was reorganized and expanded, while by the
act of September 15, 1789, its name was changed to
the Department of State, and the title of the head
became Secretary of State. Jay, who had been

appointed Chief-Justice, remained in charge, under his commission as Secretary of Foreign Affairs, till March 22, 1790, when Jefferson entered upon his duties as Secretary of State. Below is a list of the Presidents and Secretaries of State. It will be observed that there are frequent gaps between the terms of service of the Secretaries of State. These gaps were filled by *ad interim* designations, usually of some member of the cabinet, or of the chief clerk of the Department of State, or later of an assistant secretary, to perform the duties of the office.

PRESIDENTS	SECRETARIES OF STATE
George Washington, April 30, 1789, to March 3, 1797.	Thomas Jefferson, commissioned Sept. 26, 1789; entered on duties March 22, 1790; served till Dec. 31, 1793.
	Edmund Randolph, Jan. 2, 1794, to Aug. 20, 1795.
	Timothy Pickering, Dec. 10, 1795,—
John Adams, March 4, 1797, to March 3, 1801.	Timothy Pickering (continued) to May 12, 1800.
	John Marshall, May 13, 1800, to March 4, 1801.
Thomas Jefferson, March 4, 1801, to March 3, 1809.	James Madison, March 5, 1801, to March 3, 1809.
James Madison, March 4, 1809, to March 3, 1817.	Robert Smith, March 6, 1809, to April 1, 1811.
	James Monroe, April 2, 1811, to March 3, 1817.
James Monroe, March 4, 1817, to March 3, 1825.	John Quincy Adams, commissioned March 5, 1817; entered on duties Sept. 22, 1817; served to March 3, 1825.

CONDUCT OF FOREIGN INTERCOURSE

PRESIDENTS	SECRETARIES OF STATE
John Quincy Adams, March 4, 1825, to March 3, 1829.	Henry Clay, March 7, 1825, to March 3, 1829.
Andrew Jackson, March 4, 1829, to March 3, 1837.	Martin Van Buren, March 6, 1829, to May 23, 1831.
	Edward Livingston, May 24, 1831, to May 29, 1833.
	Louis McLane, May 29, 1833, to June 30, 1834.
	John Forsyth, June 27, 1834,—
Martin Van Buren, March 4, 1837, to March 3, 1841.	John Forsyth (continued) to March 3, 1841.
William Henry Harrison, March 4, 1841, to April 4, 1841.	Daniel Webster, March 5, 1841,—
John Tyler, April 6, 1841, to March 3, 1845.	Daniel Webster (continued) to May 8, 1843.
	Abel P. Upshur, July 24, 1843, to Feb. 28, 1844.
	John C. Calhoun, March 6, 1844, to March 10, 1845.
James K. Polk, March 4, 1845, to March 3, 1849.	James Buchanan, commissioned March 6, 1845; entered on duties March 10, 1845; served to March 7, 1849.
Zachary Taylor, March 5, 1849, to July 9, 1850.	John M. Clayton, March 7, 1849,—
Millard Fillmore, July 10, 1850, to March 3, 1853.	John M. Clayton (continued) to July 22, 1850.
	Daniel Webster, July 22, 1850, to Oct. 24, 1852.
	Edward Everett, Nov. 6, 1852, to March 3, 1853.
Franklin Pierce, March 4, 1853, to March 3, 1857.	William L. Marcy, March 7, 1853, to March 6, 1857.
James Buchanan, March 4, 1857, to March 3, 1861.	Lewis Cass, March 6, 1857, to Dec. 14, 1860.
	Jeremiah S. Black, Dec. 17, 1860, to March 6, 1861.
Abraham Lincoln, March 4, 1861, to April 15, 1865.	William H. Seward, March 5, 1861,—

CONDUCT OF FOREIGN INTERCOURSE

PRESIDENTS	SECRETARIES OF STATE
Andrew Johnson, April 15, 1865, to March 3, 1869.	William H. Seward (continued) to March 4, 1869.
Ulysses S. Grant, March 4, 1869, to March 3, 1877.	Elihu B. Washburne, March 5, 1869, to March 16, 1869.
	Hamilton Fish, commissioned March 11, 1869; entered on duties March 17, 1869; served to March 12, 1877.
Rutherford B. Hayes, March 5, 1877, to March 3, 1881.	William M. Evarts, March 12, 1877, to March 7, 1881.
James A. Garfield, March 4, 1881, to Sept. 19, 1881.	James G. Blaine, commissioned March 5, 1881; entered on duties March 7, 1881,—
Chester A. Arthur, Sept. 20, 1881, to March 3, 1885.	James G. Blaine (continued) to Dec. 19, 1881.
	Frederick T. Frelinghuysen, commissioned Dec. 12, 1881; entered on duties Dec. 19, 1881; served to March 6, 1885.
Grover Cleveland, March 4, 1885, to March 3, 1889.	Thomas F. Bayard, March 6, 1885, to March 6, 1889.
Benjamin Harrison, March 4, 1889, to March 3, 1893.	James G. Blaine, March 5, 1889, to June 4, 1892.
	John W. Foster, June 29, 1892, to Feb. 23, 1893.
Grover Cleveland, March 4, 1893, to March 3, 1897.	Walter Q. Gresham, March 6, 1893, to May 28, 1895.
	Richard Olney, June 8, 1895, to March 5, 1897.
William McKinley, March 4, 1897, to Sept. 14, 1901.	John Sherman, March 5, 1897, to April 25, 1898.
	William R. Day, April 26, 1898, to Sept. 16, 1898.
	John Hay, Sept, 20, 1898,—
Theodore Roosevelt, Sept. 14, 1901,——	John Hay (continued) to July 1, 1905.
	Elihu Root, July 7, 1905,—

AMERICAN DIPLOMACY

AMERICAN DIPLOMACY

ITS SPIRIT AND ACHIEVEMENTS

I

THE BEGINNINGS

WE hazard nothing in saying that not only the most important event of the past two hundred years, but one of the most important events of all time, was the advent of the United States of America into the family of nations. Its profound significance was not then unfelt, but in the nature of things its far-reaching effects could not be foreseen. Even now, as we survey the momentous changes of the last few years, we seem to stand only on the threshold of American history, as if its domain were the future rather than the past. But the splendor of the hour, while it illuminates the present, darkens by its light what lies beyond the immediate range of vision. The power which we hold to-day is no sudden and isolated possession. Its foundations were laid in the work of the original builders; and if we would understand the greatness of the present we must recur to what has gone before. Many nations have come and gone, and have left little impress upon the life of humanity. The Declaration of American Independence, however, bore upon its face the marks of distinction, and presaged the development of a theory and a policy which must be worked out in opposition to the ideas that then dominated the civilized world. Of this theory and policy the key-note was freedom; freedom of the individual, in order that he might work out his destiny in his own way; freedom in government, in order that the human faculties might have free course; freedom in commerce, in order that the resources of the earth might be developed and rendered fruitful in the increase of human wealth, contentment, and happiness.

When our ancestors embarked on the sea of independence, they were hemmed in by a system of monopolies. It was to the effects of this system that the American revolt against British authority was primarily due; and of the monopolies under which they chafed, the most galling was the commercial. It is an inevitable result of the vital connection between bodily wants and human happiness that political evils should seem to be more or less speculative so long as they do not prevent the individual from obtaining an abundance of the things that are essential to his physical comfort. This truth the system of commercial monopoly brutally disregarded. From the discovery of America and of the passage to the Eastern seas, colonies were held by the European nations only for purposes of selfish exploitation. Originally handed over to companies which possessed the exclusive right to trade with them, the principle of monopoly, even after the power of the companies was broken, was still retained. Although the English colonies were somewhat more favored than those of other nations, yet the British system, like that of the other European powers, was based upon the principle of exclusion. Foreign ships were forbidden to trade with the colonies, and many of the most important commodities could be exported only to the mother-country. British merchants likewise enjoyed the exclusive privilege of supplying the colonies with such goods as they needed from Europe. This system was rendered yet more insupportable to the American colonists by reason of the substantial liberty which they had been accustomed to exercise in matters of local government. Under what Burke described as a policy of "wise and salutary neglect," they had to a great extent been permitted to follow in such matters their own bent. But this habit of independence, practised by men in whom vigor and enterprise had been developed by life in a new world, far from reconciling them to their lot, served but to accentuate the incompatibility of commercial slavery with political freedom. The time was sure to come when colonies could no longer be treated merely as markets and as prizes of war. The American revolt was the signal of its appearance.

But there was yet another cause. The American revolt was not inspired solely by opposition to the system of commercial monopoly. The system of colonial monopoly may in a sense be said to have been but the emanation of the system of monopoly in government. In 1776 Europe for the most part was under the sway of arbitrary governments. To this rule Great Britain formed a striking exception; but even in Great Britain the struggle had barely begun which was to transform that nation into the imperial democracy of the present day. Great mutations were, however, impending in the world's political and moral order. The principles of a new philosophy were at work. With the usual human tendency to ascribe prosperity and adversity alike to the acts of government, the conviction had come to prevail that all the ills from which society suffered were ultimately to be traced to the principle of the divine right of kings, on which existing governments so generally rested. Therefore, in place of the principle of the divine right of kings, there was proclaimed the principle of the natural rights of man; and in America this principle found a congenial and unpreoccupied soil and an opportunity to grow. The theories of philosophers became in America the practice of statesmen. The

4

rights of man became the rights of individual men. Hence, our forefathers in their Declaration of Independence at the outset declared "these truths to be self-evident: that all men are created equal; that they are endowed by their Creator with certain inalienable rights; that among these are life, liberty, and the pursuit of happiness," and that "to secure these rights, governments are instituted among men, deriving their just powers from the consent of the governed."

When the United States declared their independence, they took steps to fulfil one of the necessary conditions of national life by endeavoring to enter into diplomatic relations with other powers. Indeed, even before that event, measures were taken to insure the proper conduct of foreign correspondence. On November 29, 1775, the Continental Congress appointed a committee of five, which was known as the "Committee of Secret Correspondence," for the purpose of communicating with the friends of the colonies in other parts of the world.[1] On March 3, 1776, this committee instructed Silas Deane, of Connecticut, to proceed to France in the character of a secret agent, and, if possible, to as-

[1] This committee in 1777 was denominated the "committee for foreign affairs." January 10, 1781, Congress established a "department of foreign affairs," which was to be in charge of a "Secretary of Foreign Affairs." The first incumbent of this office was Robert R. Livingston, who was appointed on August 10, 1781.

certain whether, if the colonies should be forced to form themselves into an independent state, France would probably acknowledge them as such and enter into a treaty or alliance with them for commerce or defence, or both, and if so on what conditions. These instructions were signed by Benjamin Franklin, Benjamin Harrison, John Dickinson, Robert Morris, and John Jay.

Deane's mission was by no means fruitless; but, after the Declaration of Independence, measures of a more formal kind were taken. On September 17, 1776, Congress took into consideration the subject of treaties with foreign nations, and adopted a plan of a treaty of commerce to be proposed to the King of France. Comprehensive in scope and far-reaching in its aims, this remarkable state paper stands as a monument to the broad and sagacious views of the men who framed it and gave it their sanction. Many of its provisions have found their way, often in identical terms, into the subsequent treaties of the United States; while, in its proposals for the abolition of discriminating duties that favored the native in matters of commerce and navigation, it levelled a blow at the exclusive system then prevailing, and anticipated by forty years the first successful effort to incorporate into a treaty the principle of equality and freedom on which those proposals were based. On the other hand, as if with prophetic instinct, care was taken that the expansion of the United States in the western hemisphere should not be hampered. The new government, in turning to France for aid, did not labor under misconceptions. It little detracts from our obligations to France, for support afforded us in the hour of peril and need, to say that that support was not and could not have been given by the French monarchy out of sympathy with the principles announced by the American revolutionists. No matter what incipient tendencies may have existed among the French people, there could be on the part of the French government no such sentiment. In one point, however, the French government and the French people were in feeling completely united, and that was the determination if possible to undo the results of the Seven Years' War, as embodied in the peace of Paris of 1763. Under that peace France had given to Great Britain both Canada and the Island of Cape Breton, and had practically withdrawn her flag from the Western Hemisphere. To retrieve these losses was the passionate desire of every patriotic Frenchman; and it was believed by the better - informed among our statesmen that France would overlook the act of revolt and embrace the opportunity to deal a blow at her victorious rival. Nevertheless, in the plan of a treaty to be proposed to France it was expressly declared that the Most Christian King should never invade nor attempt to possess himself of any of the countries on the continent of North America, either to the north or to the south of the United States, nor of any islands lying near that continent, except such as he might take from Great Britain in the West Indies. With this exception, the sole and perpetual possession of the countries and islands belonging to the British crown was reserved to the United States.

When this plan was adopted, Franklin, Deane, and Jefferson were chosen as commissioners to lay it before the French government; but Jefferson declined the post, and Arthur Lee, who was already in Europe, was appointed in his stead. On December 4, 1776, Franklin, weak from the effects of a tedious voyage, touched the coast of Brittany. He had just reached the Psalmist's first limit of age, and was no stranger to suffering; but, serene in the faith that sustained him in trials yet to come, he entered upon that career which was to add to his earlier renown and shed upon his borrowed years the lustre of great achievements. As soon as his health was sufficiently re-established, he hastened to Paris, where he met his colleagues in the mission; and on December 23 they jointly addressed to the Count Vergennes, then Minister of Foreign Affairs of France, the first formal diplomatic communication made on behalf of the United States to a foreign power.

The plan of a commercial treaty which the commissioners were instructed to submit proved to be unacceptable to France; nor was this strange. The

French government, while maintaining a show of neutrality, had indeed opened its treasury and its military stores to the Americans, under the guise of commercial dealings carried on through the dramatist, Beaumarchais, in the supposititious name of a Spanish firm. Nevertheless, France was still in a state of peace, her commerce unvexed by war, while America was invaded by a hostile army and her independence was yet to be established. She was free at any moment to become reconciled to England, and such a reconciliation was not deemed improbable either in England or in France. Even in America there were not wanting those who expected it. But the course of events swept the two countries rapidly along. The American commissioners, soon after they met in France, were authorized to abandon the purely commercial basis of negotiation and to propose both to France and to Spain a political connection—to the former, in return for her aid, the conquest of the West Indies; and to the latter, the subjugation of Portugal. These new instructions disclosed on the part of the United States a conviction of the necessity of foreign aid of a more direct and extensive kind than could possibly be rendered within the limits of neutrality. While the French government was still hesitating, there came the news of the surrender of Burgoyne at Saratoga. The report reached France early in December, 1777. The signal success of the American arms was the

Sir   Paris, Dec. 23. 1776

104

We beg leave to acquaint your
Excellency, that we are appointed and
fully impowered by the Congress of the
United States of America to propose
and negotiate a Treaty of Amity and
Commerce between France and the said
States. — The just and generous
Treatment their Trading Ships have
received by a free Admission into the
Ports of this Kingdom, with other consider-
rations of Respect, has induced the Con-
gress to make this Offer first to France
We

His Excell.th the Count de Vergennes

THE FIRST FORMAL DIPLOMATIC COMMUNICATION MADE ON

We request an Audience of your Excell[ency] wherein we may have an Opportunity of presenting our Credentials; and we flatter ourselves, that the Propositions we are instructed to make, are such as will not be found unacceptable

    With the greatest Regard we have the Honour to be,

        Your Excellency's most obedient and most humble Servants

        B. Franklin
        Silas Deane
        Arthur Lee

BEHALF OF THE UNITED STATES TO A FOREIGN POWER

turning-point in the negotiations. The American commissioners at once assumed a bolder front. They formally proposed a treaty of alliance, and insisted on knowing the intentions of the French court. The answer of France came on December 17. On that day the American commissioners were informed, by order of the King, that his Majesty had determined to acknowledge the independence of the United States and to make with them a treaty. The negotiations then rapidly proceeded; and on February 6, 1778, there were signed two treaties, one of commerce and the other of alliance. The commercial treaty was the one first signed, and it thus became the first treaty concluded between the United States and a foreign power. The treaty of alliance was signed immediately afterwards. The table on which these acts were performed is still preserved in the French Foreign Office.

In the treaty of commerce, the original views of the United States as to the opening of the colonial trade and the abolition of discriminating duties were by no means carried out; but the terms actually obtained embodied the most-favored-nation principle, and were as liberal as could reasonably have been expected. The treaty of alliance was, however, of a totally different nature, and established between the two countries an intimate association in respect of their foreign affairs. No one doubted that the conclusion of the alliance meant war between France and Great Britain. France's recognition of the independence of the United States was on all sides understood to be an act of intervention, which the British government would resent and oppose; for, while the United States had declared their independence, they were still in the midst of the struggle actually to secure it. This fact was acknowledged in the treaty itself. Its "essential and direct end" was avowed to be "to maintain effectually the liberty, sovereignty and independence, absolute and unlimited, of the United States, as well in matters of government as of commerce"; and it was agreed that, if war between France and Great Britain should ensue, the King of France and the United States would make it a common cause and aid each other mutually with their good offices, their counsels, and their forces. The American idea as to territorial expansion was, however, preserved. The United States, in the event of seizing the remaining British possessions in North America or the Bermuda Islands, were to be permitted to bring them into the confederacy or to hold them as dependencies. The King of France renounced them forever, reserving only the right to capture and hold any British islands in or near the Gulf of Mexico. In addition to these engagements, the United States guaranteed to France the latter's existing possessions in America as well as any which she might acquire by the future treaty of peace, while France guaranteed to the

United States their independence as well as any dominions which they might obtain from Great Britain in North America or the Bermuda Islands during the war. In conclusion, the contracting parties agreed to invite or admit other powers who had received injuries from England to make common cause with them. This stipulation particularly referred to Spain, France's intimate ally.

The French alliance was beyond all comparison the most important diplomatic event of the American Revolution. It secured to the United States, at a critical moment, the inestimable support of a power which at one time controlled the destinies of Europe and which was still the principal power on the Continent. Only one other treaty was obtained by the United States prior to the peace with Great Britain, and that was the convention of amity and commerce, signed by John Adams, with representatives of their "High Mightinesses, the States-General of the United Netherlands," at The Hague, on October 8, 1782; but the Netherlands were then also at war with Great Britain, and their recognition, though most timely and helpful, was not of vital import. The failure, however, to make other treaties was not due to any lack of effort. Agents were accredited by the Continental Congress to various courts in Europe. John Jay and William Carmichael were sent to Spain; Ralph Izard was appointed to Tuscany; William Lee was directed to test

14

JOHN ADAMS

the disposition of Vienna; Arthur Lee was authorized to sound various courts, including that of Prussia; Francis Dana was bidden to knock at the door of Russia; Henry Laurens was commissioned to the Netherlands. The fortunes and misfortunes of some of these agents form a curious chapter.

There exists a popular tendency to overrate the delights and to underrate the hardships of the diplomatic life; but, however much opinions may differ on this point, there can be no doubt that the office of an American diplomatist in the days of the Revolution was no holiday pastime. If he was not already in Europe, his journey to his post was beset with perils graver than those of the elements. In the eyes of British law, American revolutionists were simply "rebels," the reprobation of whose conduct was likely to be proportioned to their prominence and activity; and the seas were scoured by British cruisers, the dreaded embodiment of England's maritime supremacy. Deane went abroad secretly before independence was declared; but when his presence in France became known, the British government asked that he be seized and delivered up into its custody. Franklin sailed for France on a small vessel of war belonging to Congress, called the *Reprisal*. On the way over she took two prizes, and more than once, descrying a suspicious sail, cleared for action. Had she been captured by the British, Franklin would have had an opportunity to test the truth of his remark to his associates in Congress, that they must "either hang together or hang separately." Not long after bearing Franklin to France, the *Reprisal* went down with her gallant commander, Captain Wickes, off the banks of New-foundland. John Adams, on his first journey, took passage on an American vessel; on his second, he embarked in the French frigate *Sensible*, and landed at Ferrol, in Spain. Jay committed his fate to the American man-of-war *Confederacy*, and, like Adams and Franklin, reached his destination. Less fortu-nate was Henry Laurens.

Laurens was elected minister to the Netherlands in October, 1779, but, owing to the vigilance of the British watch of the American coasts, did not sail till August, 1780, when he took passage on a small packet-boat called the *Mercury*, under the convoy of the sloop-of-war *Saratoga*. When off the banks of Newfoundland, the *Mercury*, then abandoned by her convoy, was chased and seized by the British cruiser *Vestal*. During the pursuit, Laurens's pa-pers were hastily put into a bag, with "a reasonable weight of iron shot," and thrown overboard. The weight, however, was not sufficient to sink them, and they fell into the hands of the captors, by whom they were "hooked up" and delivered to the Brit-ish government. Laurens himself was imprisoned in the Tower of London. Never did consequences more momentous flow from a confused effort to sup-

ply the want of previous precautions. Among the
papers there was a tentative plan of a commercial
treaty between the United States and the Netherlands, which William Lee had, on September 4,
1778, agreed upon with Van Berckel, Grand Pension-
ary of Amsterdam, who had been authorized by the
burgomasters to treat. Obviously this act was in
no wise binding upon the States-General, and Van
Berckel had formally declared that the treaty was
not to be concluded till the independence of the
United States should be recognized by the English.
But trouble had long been brewing between the
English and the Dutch; and the British minister at
The Hague was instructed to demand the disavowal
of the treaty, and the punishment of Van Berckel
and his "accomplices" as "disturbers of the public
peace and violators of the law of nations." This
demand the Dutch declined to grant; and on December 20, 1780, the British government proclaimed
general reprisals.

While the persons of our representatives were
safe from seizure upon the Continent, they obtained
no substantial recognition outside of France and
the Netherlands. In 1777 Arthur Lee was stopped
by the Spanish government when on his way to
Madrid. Jay and William Carmichael were afterwards allowed to reside there, but only as private
individuals. In the early days of the Revolution,
Spain had given some pecuniary aid at the solicita-

tion of France. That Congress expected to obtain from her further assistance may be inferred from the circumstance that Jay had scarcely left the United States when bills were drawn upon him to a large amount. But, with the exception of an insignificant sum, insufficient to enable him to meet these bills, which Franklin had ultimately to take up, Jay obtained no aid and made no progress. With regard to the Mississippi, Spain demanded an exclusive navigation; but, in spite of the fact that Congress, against Jay's warning that such a course would render a future war with Spain unavoidable, eventually offered in return for an alliance to concede this demand from 31° of north latitude southward, his mission failed. Spain ultimately went to war against Great Britain, but for her own purposes. With a presentiment not unnatural, she to the end regretted the independence of the United States. In a prophetic paper submitted to the Spanish King, after peace was re-established, Count d'Aranda, who was Spanish ambassador at Paris during the American Revolution, said: "The independence of the English colonies has been recognized. It is for me a subject of grief and fear. France has but few possessions in America, but she was bound to consider that Spain, her most intimate ally, had many, and that she now stands exposed to terrible reverses. From the beginning, France has acted against her true interests in encouraging and sup-

porting this independence, and so I have often declared to the ministers of that nation."

While the attitude of Spain towards the Revolution was affected by considerations of her particular interests, it was to a great extent shared by
most of the powers of Europe. William Lee went
to Vienna, but was not received there. Dana resided
for two years at St. Petersburg as a private individual, and obtained nothing beyond one informal interview with the Minister of Foreign Affairs. Izard
was dissuaded by the minister of Tuscany, at Paris,
from attempting to visit that country, and ended
his diplomatic career in unhappy discontent at the
French capital. But the greatest misfortune of all
was that which befell Arthur Lee at the Prussian
capital.

Diplomacy, in the course of time, had lost much
of its idle pomp and ceremony, but had gained little
in scrupulousness and delicacy. Bribery was still
one of its most formidable weapons; but in its treatment of Lee it also employed methods the burgla-
rious grossness of which was mollified only by the
histrionic air that pervaded the whole transaction.
Great concern was felt by England as to the possible course of Prussia; and when, early in May,
1777, the British government received, through one
of its ubiquitous agencies, a report that Lee and
Carmichael were about to proceed from Paris to
Berlin, the Earl of Suffolk directed Hugh Elliot, the

British minister at the latter capital, to "give every proper attention to their conduct, and the impression which it may make." His lordship added, with that completeness and accuracy of information which characterized all his communications, that Carmichael had "the best abilities," but that Lee was more immediately in the commission of Congress. At the end of May, his lordship wrote that a Mr. Sayre, and not Carmichael, would accompany Lee to Berlin; and Sayre he described as "a man of desperate private fortune, but with the disposition rather than the talents to be mischievous." Sayre was in fact one of those adventurers with whom Lee, through bad judgment, permitted himself often to be associated, with unhappy results. Meanwhile, before Elliot could have received his lordship's second letter, all diplomatic Berlin was agog over the arrival of Lee and a "Mr. Stephens," such being the patronymic under which Sayre, whose Christian name was Stephen, then travelled, while he assumed the character of a banker. Elliot, however, was not deceived; and, with the ardent desire of a young man of twenty-four to show his mettle, he set about his task with diligence and enthusiasm. His suspicions were soon inflamed by learning that Lee had had a private interview with Count Schulenburg and was in correspondence with him, and that Herr Zegelin, formerly Prussian minister at Constantinople, who was supposed to be much employed by

Frederick the Great in confidential negotiations, had come to Berlin "unexpectedly," and taken lodgings not only in the same inn with Lee and Sayre, but even on the same floor. Nor was Elliot reassured when Count Schulenburg, on a certain occasion, turned the conversation to the "report" of the arrival of the "Americans," for the purpose of saying that he knew nothing of it; nor when, still later, he admitted that they had proposed to sell some tobacco at a low price, but declared that the King was "entirely ignorant of their being at all connected with the rebels in America." Elliot, however, had determined to get authentic information at first hand. Through a German servant in his employ, he "gained," as he expressed it, the co-operation of the servants at the inn and of the landlord's wife. By this means he learned that Lee kept his papers, including a journal of each day's transactions, in a portfolio which was usually laid away in a bureau. He therefore had false keys made, both to the door of the chamber and the bureau; and having learned that on a certain day Lee and Sayre were going into the country, where they usually stayed till eleven at night, he sent his German servant to bring away the papers. When the servant reached the inn, some strangers had just arrived, and as he could not enter the door without being seen, he got into Lee's room through a window. He returned with the portfolio about four o'clock. Elliot was at dinner, duly provided with four guests, "who were all enjoined to the most sacred secrecy, and set to copying instantly," while he himself went about to pay visits and show himself. He was still thus engaged when, calling about eight o'clock at the inn on pretence of seeing a fellow-countryman, Lord Russborough, he found that Lee and Sayre had just arrived. He then assumed the most difficult part of his task. Knowing that the papers had not been returned, he, in company with Russborough, joined Lee and Sayre and endeavored to amuse them with conversation, which he did for nearly two hours, without any introductions, or any disclosure of names, but merely as one who had happened to meet persons speaking the same language. At ten o'clock, however, Lee retired, saying that he must go to his room and write. Soon afterwards Elliot heard a "violent clamor" in the house of a "robbery" and "loss of papers." He then drove home, and, finding most of the papers copied, disguised himself and took them to the mistress of the house, who, being in the plot, told the story that they were left at the door by some one who announced their return through the keyhole and then ran off. Lee appealed to the police, and an inquiry was promptly set on foot. It soon led to the German servant. Elliot, who was not unprepared for this contingency, immediately sent him out of the country, and made to the Prussian government, as well as to his own, an official explanation of the incident. According to this version, the affair was altogether an accident, due to his own imprudence in saying in the presence of an over-officious servant, that he would give a large sum of money to see Mr. Lee's papers; but, as soon as the "unwarrantable action" of the servant was discovered, the papers were returned. This account naturally found little credence, although diplomatic opinion of the merits of the transaction was said to be much "divided." But the knowledge of the fact that the British government had obtained copies of Lee's papers put an end to the attempt privately to negotiate with the Prussian government, and frustrated the plans for obtaining supplies from Prussian ports.

In the narration of the course of our Revolutionary diplomacy, there yet remains to be mentioned one name, that of Charles William Frederick Dumas. To the people of the United States it is to-day practically unknown; but I do not hesitate to affirm that, with the exception of Adams, Franklin, and Jay, he rendered to the American cause in Europe services more important than did any other man. A native of Switzerland, though he spent most of his life in the Netherlands; a man "of deep learning, versed in the ancient classics, and skilled in several modern languages"; the author and translator of a large number of works, some of which related to America, and the editor of an edition of Vattel, with a preface and copious notes—he felt at the very beginning the inspiration of the American cause, and from thenceforth dedicated his all to its advancement. When the first report of the Revolution was heard in Europe, he began to employ his pen in its support. Besides publishing and circulating an explanation of its causes, he translated and spread abroad the proceedings of the Continental Congress. Towards the end of 1775, his services were solicited by Franklin, in the name of the Committee of Secret Correspondence, as an agent of the American colonies in the Netherlands. He accepted the commission with the promise of "a hearty good-will and an untiring zeal," adding: "This promise on my part is in fact an oath of allegiance, which I spontaneously take to Congress." Never was oath more faithfully kept. His voluminous reports to Congress, some of which have been published, attest his constant activity. He journeyed from city to city, and from state to state, in the Low Countries, as the apostle of American independence. He lent his aid to Adams as secretary and translator, and later acted as *chargé d'affaires*, exchanging in that capacity for the United States the ratifications of the treaty which Adams had concluded with the Dutch government. And if, when the treaty was made, it represented not merely a perception of material interests, but the sentiment of fraternity commemorated in the medals of the time, the fact was in no small measure due to the untiring devotion of this neglected advocate of the American cause, to whom some memorial should yet be raised in recognition of his zeal, his sacrifices, and his deserts.

We have seen that in diplomacy, in spite of its supposed precautions, chance often plays an important part. So it happened in the case of the negotiations between England and America for peace. In the winter of 1781–82, a friend and neighbor of Franklin's, Madame Brillon, met at Nice a number of the English gentry. Among these was Lord Cholmondeley, who promised while on his return to England to call upon Franklin and drink tea with him at Passy. On March 21, 1782, Franklin received a note from his lordship, who, in the interview that followed, offered to bear a note to Lord Shelburne, who, as he assured Franklin, felt for him a high regard. Franklin accepted the suggestion and wrote a brief letter, in which he expressed a wish that a "general peace" might be brought about, though he betrayed no hope that it would soon take place. But at this moment the political situation in England was somewhat tumultuous. The American war was becoming more and more unpopular; and on March 20th Lord North resigned. In this emergency George III. sent for Lord Shelburne. Shelburne advised that Lord Rockingham be called to the head of the cabinet, and declared the recognition of American independence to be indispensable.

Rockingham was made Prime-Minister, and Shelburne became Secretary for Home and Colonial Affairs. The Foreign Office was given to Charles James Fox. Franklin's letter to Shelburne was written without knowledge of the significant change then taking place in the British ministry. Soon afterwards news came of Shelburne's entrance into the cabinet; but Franklin thought no more of his letter till the second week in April, when a neighbor appeared and introduced a Mr. Oswald, who after some conversation handed Franklin two letters, one from Shelburne and the other from Henry Laurens. The letter from Shelburne, besides commending Oswald as an honest and capable man, expressed his lordship's desire to retain between himself and Franklin the same simplicity and good faith which had subsisted between them in transactions of less importance.

Although Fox has always been regarded with affection in America as a friend of the colonists, it was fortunate that the negotiations fell into the hands of Shelburne. Associated in his earlier career with men of reactionary tendencies, he afterwards became an eminent representative of the liberal economic school of which Adam Smith was the founder. As often happens, this change in his position gave rise to suspicions as to his sincerity. Lacking the vehemence which characterized Fox, and which gives even to the most flexible conduct the

air of passionate sincerity, Shelburne was a man of
high intellectual power, who followed the dictates
of reason rather than the impulses of feeling. No
better evidence could be adduced of the sincerity
of his desire to treat on the most liberal basis than his
choice of Richard Oswald as a negotiator. Ingen-
uous and impulsive, in the end the British cabinet
was obliged to send an assistant to withdraw some
of his concessions. On the part of the United States,
authority to negotiate for peace had been given to
Adams, Franklin, Jay, and Laurens. Jay arrived
in Paris late in June, 1782, and for a time thereafter,
owing to the illness of Franklin, the negotiations fell
chiefly into his hands. But on July 6th Franklin
presented to Oswald certain propositions, three of
which were put forward as necessary, and two as
advisable. The former were (1) the acknowledg-
ment of independence, (2) a settlement of the boundaries, and (3) freedom of fishing; the advisable stipulations were (1) free commercial intercourse and (2)
the cession of the province of Canada to the United
States, partly in payment of war claims and partly
to create a fund for the compensation of loyalists
whose property had been seized and confiscated.
The negotiations continued substantially on these
lines till Adams, fresh from his triumphs in the
Netherlands, joined his associates in the commission.
He arrived in Paris, October 26, 1782. The British
government had then conceded (1) independence,

(2) a settlement of the boundaries, (3) the restriction of Canada to its ancient limits, and (4) freedom of fishing on the banks of Newfoundland and elsewhere. There still remained open the questions (1) of the right to dry fish on the British coasts, (2) the payment of debts due to British subjects prior to the war, and (3) the compensation of the loyalists. To the last measure Franklin was unalterably opposed, and whenever it was pressed brought up his proposition for the cession of Canada. Adams was equally insistent upon the right of drying and curing fish on the British coasts. The question as to the payment of debts grew out of the acts of sequestration passed by certain States during the Revolution for the purpose of causing debts due to British creditors to be paid into the public treasuries. The lawfulness of this transaction became a subject of controversy in the peace negotiations, especially in connection with the claims of the loyalists for compensation for their confiscated estates. Franklin and Jay, though they deprecated the policy of confiscating private debts, hesitated on the ground of a want of authority in the existing national government to override the acts of the States. But, by one of those dramatic strokes of which he was a master, John Adams, when he arrived on the scene, ended the discussion by suddenly declaring, in the presence of the British plenipotentiaries, that he "had no notion of cheating anybody"; and that,

while he was opposed to compensating the loyalists, he would agree to a stipulation to enable the British creditors to sue for the recovery of their debts. Such a stipulation was inserted in the treaty. It is remarkable not only as the embodiment of an enlightened policy, but also as the strongest assertion in the acts of that time of the power and authority of the national government. The final concession as to the fisheries was also granted upon the demand of Adams, who declared that he would not sign a treaty on any other terms. Before the close of the negotiations, Henry Laurens arrived in Paris; and there, on November 30th, he joined his three colleagues in signing, with Richard Oswald, the provisional articles of peace. It has often been said that of all the treaties Great Britain ever made, this was the one by which she gave the most and took the least. It brought, however, upon Shelburne and his associates the censure of the House of Commons, and caused the downfall of his ministry.

The articles were signed by the American commissioners without consultation with the French government. In taking this course, the commissioners acted in opposition to their instructions. Their action was due to suspicions first entertained by Jay, but in which Adams, who besides was little disposed to defer to Vergennes, participated. Franklin, although he does not appear to have shared the feelings of his colleagues, determined to act with them. The question whether they were justified has given rise to controversies perhaps more voluminous than important. Every source of information has been diligently explored in order to ascertain whether the suspicions of Jay were, in fact, well or ill founded. This test does not, however, seem to be necessarily conclusive. In law, the justification of an act often depends not so much upon the actual as upon the apparent reality of the danger. The principal ground of Jay's distrust was a secret mission to England of Rayneval, an *attaché* of the French Foreign Office, and an especial representative of Vergennes. Jay suspected that Rayneval had been sent to London to learn from Shelburne the views of the American commissioners, and to assure him of the support of France if he should reject their claims to the fisheries and the Mississippi. The disclosure in recent years of Rayneval's reports to Vergennes has shown that his mission had other objects, though it is no doubt also true that the government of France, mindful of its own historic contentions, as well as of the interests of its other ally, Spain, regarded the claims of the Americans as excessive and was indisposed to support them. But whether the conduct of the American commissioners was or was not justifiable, it aroused the indignation of the French government. "You are about to hold out," wrote Vergennes to Franklin, "a certain hope of peace to America without even informing yourself of the state of negotiations on our part. You are wise and discreet, sir; you perfectly understand what is due to propriety; you have all your life performed your duties. I pray you to consider how you propose to fulfil those which are due to the King. I am not desirous of enlarging these reflections. I recommend them to your own integrity." No paper that Franklin ever wrote displays his marvellous skill to more advantage than his reply to these reproaches. While protesting that nothing had been agreed in the preliminaries contrary to the interests of France, he admitted that the American commissioners had "been guilty of neglecting a point of *bienséance*." But as this was not, he declared, from want of respect to the King, whom they all loved and honored, he hoped that it would be excused, and that "the great work, which has hitherto been so happily conducted, is so nearly brought to perfection, and is so glorious to his reign, will not be ruined by a single indiscretion of ours." And then he adds this adroit suggestion: "*The English, I just now learn, flatter themselves they have already divided us.* I hope this little misunderstanding will therefore be kept a secret, and that they will find themselves totally mistaken."

When the provisional articles of peace were signed, the American commissioners hoped subsequently to be able to conclude a commercial arrangement.

This hope proved to be delusive. On September 3, 1783, the provisional articles were formally converted into a definitive peace. The old system, embodied in the Navigation Act, England even yet was not ready to abandon. It still dominated Europe, and confined the New World outside of the United States. Years of strife were to ensue before it was to fall to pieces; and in the course of the conflict the United States was to stand as the exponent and defender of neutral rights and commercial freedom.

II

THE SYSTEM OF NEUTRALITY

BETWEEN 1776, when independence was proclaimed, and 1789, when the government under the Constitution was inaugurated, the United States entered into fourteen treaties — six with France, three with Great Britain, two with the Netherlands, and one each with Sweden, Prussia, and Morocco; but a majority of all were negotiated and signed in France, at Paris or at Versailles. Eight were subscribed, on the part of the United States, by two or more plenipotentiaries; and among their names we find, either alone or in association, that of Franklin, ten times; the name of Adams, seven times; that of Jefferson, three times; and that of Jay, twice. These early treaties covered a wide range of subjects, embracing not only war and peace, and, as did those with France, political alliance, but also commercial intercourse and the rights of consuls. Among their various stipulations, we find provisions for liberty of conscience, and for the removal of the disability of aliens in respect of their property and their business. Stipulations for the mitigation of the evils of war are numerous. A fixed time is allowed, in the unfortunate event of hostilities, for the sale or withdrawal of goods; provision is made for the humane treatment of prisoners of war; the exercise of visit and search at sea is regulated and restrained; the acceptance by a citizen of the one country of a privateering commission from the enemy of the other is assimilated to piracy; and an effort is made to limit the scope of belligerent captures at sea. But, prior to the establishment of the Constitution, it was easier for the United States to make treaties than to enforce them. In spite of the engagement of the treaty of peace, that his Britannic Majesty should with "all convenient speed" withdraw his "armies, garrisons and fleets" from the United States, important posts within the northern frontier continued to be occupied by the British forces; and when the government of the United States protested, the British government pointed to the refusal of the State courts to respect the treaty pledge that British creditors should meet with no lawful impediment to the recovery of their confiscated debts. For similar reasons, the act of the United States in sending John Adams, soon after the peace, as minister to the court of St. James, remained unreciprocated.

The termination of the period of divergence and of incapacity for uniform action among the several States came none too soon. Perils were close at hand, the disruptive impulses of which the old confederation could not have withstood. They were even to test the efficacy of the new Constitution. In 1789, when that instrument was put into operation, France was in the first throes of the great revolution which was eventually to involve all Europe in a struggle of unprecedented magnitude and severity. What attitude was the United States to hold towards this impending conflict? Even apart from the treaties with France of 1778, the question was fraught with grave possibilities. For generations, Europe had been a vast battle-ground, on which had been fought out the contests not only for political but also for commercial supremacy. Of the end of these contests, there appeared to be no sign; nor, in spite of their long continuance, had the rights and duties of non-participant or neutral nations been clearly and comprehensively defined. Indeed, so intricate were the ramifications of the European system that, when discords arose, it seemed to afford little room for neutrality. The situation of the United States was essentially different. Physically remote from the Old World, its political interests also were detached from those of Europe. Except as it might be drawn into disputes affecting the fate of existing colonies or the formation of new ones in America, it was not likely to become embroiled in European wars. Not only, therefore, did it enjoy the opportunity to be neutral, but its permanent interest appeared to be that of neutrality; and the importance of preserving this interest was greatly enhanced by the necessity of commercial and industrial development. The new nation, though born, was yet to demonstrate to a world somewhat sceptical and not altogether friendly its right and its power to live and to grow. It was easy to foresee that its enterprise would penetrate to the farthest corners of the globe, and that its commerce, overspreading the seas, would be exposed to hazards and vexations of which the most uncertain and potentially the most disastrous were those arising from the exorbitant pretensions of belligerents. To resist these pretensions would fall to the lot of a neutral power; and upon the results of this resistance would depend the right to be independent in reality as well as in name, and to enjoy the incidents of independence.

In circumstances such as these it is not strange that Washington and his advisers watched with anxiety the progress of the French Revolution, as, growing in intensity and in violence, it encountered, first, the agitated disapprobation, and then the frantic opposition of other powers. It was not till 1793, when England entered into the conflict, that the war, by assuming a distinctively maritime form, raised a question as to the obligations of the United States under the treaties with France; but, long prior to that event, popular feeling in America was deeply stirred. Although the treaties of 1778 were

made with Louis XVI., yet in the sounds of the
French Revolution the American people discerned a
reverberation of their own immortal declaration.
From Boston to Savannah, there were manifestations of the liveliest sympathy and enthusiasm. To
set bounds to this tendency, obviously would require
the exercise of unusual prudence and firmness on the
part of those intrusted with the affairs of government. America had fought for freedom, but her
statesmen were not mere doctrinaires. Their aims
were practical. They understood that the peaceful demonstration of the beneficence of their principles, in producing order, prosperity, and contentment at home, was likely to accomplish far more for
the cause of liberty than an armed propagandism,
which perchance might ultimately degenerate into
military despotism. It was therefore important to
avoid premature commitments. To a perception
of this fact is no doubt to be ascribed the appointment by Washington, on January 12, 1792, of
Gouverneur Morris as minister to France. In his
own country Morris had been a supporter of the
Revolution, a member of the Continental Congress,
assistant to Robert Morris in the management of
the public finances, and a member of the Constitutional Convention of 1787. From the beginning,
however, he had exhibited a distrust of the revolution in France. He instinctively recoiled from the
excesses that were committed when his forebodings

came to be fulfilled. Before he became minister of the United States, he offered his counsel to Louis XVI., in a sense directly antagonistic to the Revolution; and he afterwards sought to effect that monarch's escape. Such a man could not be acceptable to the revolutionary leaders; but he at any rate possessed an intimate knowledge of the conditions and tendencies of the time, and was not likely to commit his government to extravagant policies.

Early in 1793 a new minister was appointed by France to the United States. His name was Edmond C. Genêt. Of Morris he was in many respects the precise antithesis; for, while by no means destitute of experience, he was a turbulent champion of the new order of things. According to his own account, he was placed at the age of twelve years in the French Foreign Office, where, under the direction of his father, he translated into French a number of American political writings. After spending seven years at the head of a bureau at Versailles, under the direction of Vergennes, he passed one year at London, two years at Vienna, one at Berlin, and five in Russia. At St. Petersburg, however, he fell into difficulties. Because of some of his representations, which were pitched too high in the revolutionary scale, the Empress Catherine requested his recall, and, when it was refused, dismissed him. In reporting his departure for the United States, Morris observed that "the pompousness of this embassy

could not but excite the attention of England."
What it was that called forth this remark does not
appear; but, whatever it may have been, there can
be no doubt that Genêt set out on his mission gur-
gling with the fermentation of the new wine of the
Revolution; and he had scarcely left France when
Morris reported that the Executive Council had sent
out by him three hundred blank commissions for
privateers, to be distributed among such persons as
might be willing to fit out vessels in the United States
to prey on British commerce.

On April 18, 1793, before this report was received,
Washington submitted to the various members of
his cabinet a series of questions touching the relations between the United States and France. These
questions were, first, whether a proclamation of
neutrality should issue; second, whether a minister
from the republic of France should be received;
third, whether, if received, he should be received
unconditionally or with qualifications; fourth,
whether the treaties previously made with France
were to be considered as still in force. At a meeting of the cabinet, on April 19th, it was determined,
with the concurrence of all the members, that a
proclamation of neutrality should issue, and that
the minister from the French Republic should be
received. On the third question, Hamilton, who
was Secretary of the Treasury, was supported by
Knox, the Secretary of War, in the opinion that the

reception should be qualified, while Washington, Jefferson, his Secretary of State, and Randolph, the Attorney-General, inclined to the opposite view; but the third and fourth questions were postponed for further consideration. In a subsequent written opinion Hamilton argued that the reception of Genêt should be qualified by an express reservation of the question whether the treaties were not to be deemed temporarily and provisionally suspended by reason of the radical change in conditions since they were formed. He also thought the war plainly offensive on the part of France, while the alliance was defensive. On the other hand, Jefferson maintained that the treaties were not "between the United States and Louis Capet, but between the two nations of America and France," and that "the nations remaining in existence, though both of them have since changed their forms of government, the treaties are not annulled by these changes." He also contended that the reception of a minister had nothing to do with this question.

On April 22, 1793, Washington issued his famous proclamation of neutrality. On April 8th, just two weeks before, Genêt had arrived at Charleston, South Carolina; but the news of his presence there reached Philadelphia through the public press only on the day on which the proclamation was published. At Charleston he lost no time in fitting-out and commissioning privateers; and, after having got

22ᵈ April, 1793.

By the PRESIDENT of the United States of America.

A PROCLAMATION.

WHEREAS it appears that a ſtate of war exiſts between Auſtria, Pruſſia, Sardinia, Great-Britain, and the United Netherlands, of the one part, and France on the other, and the duty and intereſt of the United States require, that they ſhould with ſincerity and good faith adopt and purſue a conduct friendly and impartial toward the belligerent powers:

I have therefore thought fit by theſe preſents to declare the diſpoſition of the United States to obſerve the conduct aforeſaid towards thoſe powers reſpectively; and to exhort and warn the citizens of the United States carefully to avoid all acts and proceedings whatſoever, which may in any manner tend to contravene ſuch diſpoſition.

And I do hereby alſo make known that whoſoever of the citizens of the United States ſhall render himſelf liable to puniſhment or forfeiture under the law of nations, by committing, aiding or abetting hoſtilities againſt any of the ſaid powers, or by carrying to any of them thoſe articles, which are deemed contraband by the *modern* uſage of nations, will not receive the protection of the United States, againſt ſuch puniſhment or forfeiture : and further, that I have given inſtructions to thoſe officers, to whom it belongs, to cauſe proſecutions to be inſtituted againſt all perſons, who ſhall, within the cognizance of the courts of the United States, violate the Law of Nations, with reſpect to the powers at war, or any of them.

IN TESTIMONY WHEREOF *I have cauſed the Seal of the United States of America to be affixed to theſe preſents, and ſigned the ſame with my hand. Done at the city of Philadelphia, the twenty-ſecond day of April, one thouſand ſeven hundred and ninety-three, and of the Independence of the United States of America the ſeventeenth.*

L. S.

Gᵒ. **WASHINGTON.**

By the President.
TH: JEFFERSON.

a number ready for sea, he proceeded to the seat of the national government by land. On the way he incited the people to hostility against Great Britain, and received such demonstrations of sympathy as to strengthen his confidence in the success of the course on which he had entered.

The posture of affairs between the United States and France was complicated and difficult. By the treaty of commerce of 1778, the ships of war and privateers of the one country were entitled to enter the ports of the other with their prizes, without being subjected to any examination as to their law-fulness, while cruisers of the enemy were in like cir-cumstances to be excluded, unless in case of stress of weather. By the treaty of alliance, the United States, as has been seen, had guaranteed to France her possessions in America. For the moment, how-ever, the situation was much simplified by reason of the fact that the French Republic did not ask of the United States the execution of the territorial guarantee. This may be accounted for by either of two reasons. The general arming of the whole popu-lation and the exhaustive devotion of the resources of the country to military purposes had caused a scarcity in France both of money and of provisions. The United States, as a neutral, formed a source of supply of both. An intimation to this effect was made by the French government to Morris not long before the issuance of Washington's proclamation of neutrality; and the same idea was strongly expressed in a report of the French Minister of Foreign Affairs, in June, 1793, in which it was said that the United States became "more and more the granary of France and her colonies." But there may have been yet another reason. It is not improbable that the National Assembly, while balancing the advantages of American neutrality against those of the treaty of alliance, doubted whether the guarantee was precisely applicable to the conditions then existing. This doubt is suggested by the original instructions to Genêt, which, although they were given before the conflict with England began, were written in contemplation of hostilities with that country as well as with Spain; and in these instructions, which looked to the formation of a new commercial and political connection with the United States, adapted to the conditions which the French Revolution had produced, Genêt was directed to bring about "a national agreement, in which two great peoples shall suspend their commercial and political interests, and establish a mutual understanding to defend the empire of liberty, wherever it can be embraced."

When Genêt arrived in Philadelphia, an unqualified reception was promptly accorded him. In presenting his letters of credence, he stated that his government knew that "under present circumstances" they had a right to call upon the United

States for the guarantee of their islands, but declared that they did not desire it; in a subsequent communication, he proposed that the two peoples should, "by a true family compact, establish a commercial and political system" on a "liberal and fraternal basis." The administration, however, was indisposed to quixotic enterprises. On the contrary, it was soon fully occupied with its efforts to vindicate its proclamation of neutrality, which was constantly violated by the fitting-out of privateers, the condemnation of prizes by French consuls sitting as courts of admiralty, and even by the capture of vessels within the jurisdiction of the United States. These proceedings, in which he was himself directly implicated, Genêt defended as being in conformity not only with the treaties between the two countries, but also with the principles of neutrality. When Jefferson cited the utterances of writers on the law of nations, Genêt repelled them as "diplomatic subtleties" and as "aphorisms of Vattel and others." He especially insisted that, by the treaty of commerce of 1778, the authorities of the United States were precluded from interfering in any manner with the prizes brought into their ports by the French privateers. The United States, on the other hand, denied that the contracting parties, in agreeing that prizes should not be subject to examination as to their lawfulness, deprived themselves of the right to prevent the capture and condemnation of vessels in violation of their own neutrality and sovereignty.

In the correspondence to which these differences gave rise, Jefferson, always perspicacious in his deductions from fundamental principles, expounded with remarkable clearness and power the nature and scope of neutral duty. Its foundations he discovered in two simple conceptions—the exclusive sovereignty of the nation within its own territory and the obligation of impartiality towards belligerents. As it was "the *right* of every nation to prohibit acts of sovereignty from being exercised by any other within its limits," so it was, he declared, "the *duty* of a neutral nation to prohibit such as would injure one of the warring powers." Hence, "no succor should be given to either, unless stipulated by treaty, in men, arms, or anything else, directly serving for war." The raising of troops and the granting of military commissions were, besides, sovereign rights, which, as they pertained exclusively to the nation itself, could not be exercised within its territory by a foreign power, without its consent; and if the United States had "a right to refuse permission to arm vessels and raise men" within its ports and territories, it was "bound by the laws of neutrality to exercise that right, and to prohibit such armaments and enlistments."

Such, briefly summarized, was the theory of neutral duty formulated by Jefferson. But the administration did not stop with the enunciation of doctrines. It endowed them with vitality. Acknowledging the obligation of the government to make indemnity for any losses resulting from its previous failure to cause its neutrality to be respected, it adopted efficacious measures to prevent the future fitting-out of privateers in the ports of the United States, to exclude from asylum therein any that had been so equipped, and to cause the restitution of any prizes brought by them within the national jurisdiction. To insure the enforcement of these rules, instructions were issued by Hamilton to the collectors of customs; and on June 5, 1794, there was passed the first Neutrality Act, which forbade within the United States the acceptance and exercise of commissions, the enlistment of men, the fitting-out and arming of vessels, and the setting on foot of military expeditions, in the service of any prince or state with which the government was at peace. In due season compensation was made to British subjects for the injuries inflicted by French privateers in violation of American neutrality. "The policy of the United States in 1793," says the late W. E. Hall, one of the most eminent of English publicists, "constitutes an epoch in the development of the usages of neutrality. There can be no doubt that it was intended and believed to give effect to the obligations then incumbent on neutrals. But it represented by far the most advanced existing opin-

THOMAS JEFFERSON

ions as to what those obligations were; and in some points it even went further than authoritative custom has up to the present day advanced. In the main, however, it is identical with the standard of conduct which is now adopted by the community of nations."

Against the course of the administration Genêt did not cease to protest; and, while he was himself its first victim, his misfortunes may serve as a warning to foreign ministers who may be disposed to reckon upon popular support in opposing the government to which they are accredited. There was indeed in his case much to mislead a judgment which, no matter how honest it may have been, was not well balanced. To the superficial observer it might have seemed that there were in the United States few Americans; that the population was almost wholly composed of partisans of France and partisans of Great Britain, the former constituting a vast majority; and that the administration, which was daily assailed with a virulence that knew neither restraint nor decency, might safely be flouted and defied. But when, convinced that the proclamation of neutrality would be faithfully enforced, Genêt denounced the government for the " cowardly abandonment " of its friends, and, besides expressing contempt for the opinions of the President, persisted in questioning his authority, Morris was instructed to ask for his recall. The

French government not only granted the request, but expressed disapprobation of Genêt's "criminal proceedings"; and his successor, M. Fauchet, demanded his delivery-up for punishment. This the United States refused "upon reasons of law and magnanimity." Genêt maintained, and with much reason, that he had acted in conformity with his instructions, which in reality contemplated the organization of hostile enterprises in the United States against Spain as well as Great Britain. Nevertheless, he did not return to France, but settled in the United States, where he married the daughter of an eminent American statesman and spent the remainder of his days. It is only just to say that he has been the subject of much unmerited obloquy. In circumstances exceptionally trying, his conduct was ill-advised, but not malevolent. William Cullen Bryant, speaking in 1870, said that he remembered Genêt very vividly, as he appeared forty-five years before, when he came occasionally to the city of New York. "He was," said Bryant, "a tall man, with a reddish wig and a full, round voice, speaking English in a sort of oratorical manner, like a man making a speech, but very well for a Frenchman. He was a dreamer in some respects, and, I remember, had a plan for navigating the air in balloons. A pamphlet of his was published a little before the time I knew him, entitled 'Aërial Navigation,' illustrated by an engraving of a balloon shaped like a fish, propelled by sails and guided by a rudder, in which he maintained that man could navigate the air as well as he could navigate the ocean in a ship."

The authorities of the French Republic took advantage of the request for Genêt's recall to ask for Morris's withdrawal. Under the circumstances, this act of reciprocity was ungrudgingly conceded. Morris was succeeded in France by James Monroe.

The Neutrality Act of 1794, though originally limited in duration, was afterwards extended, and was then continued in force indefinitely. In order to meet conditions arising out of the war of the Spanish colonies in America for independence, an additional act was passed in 1817; but this, together with all prior legislation on the subject, was superseded by the comprehensive statute of April 20, 1818, the provisions of which are now embodied in the Revised Statutes of the United States. A similar act was passed by the British Parliament in the following year; laws and regulations were from time to time adopted by other governments; and the duties of neutrality became a fixed and determinate part of international law. The severest test of the system, as the ultimate standard of national obligation and responsibility, was made in the case of the claims of the United States against Great Britain generically known as the "*Alabama* Claims," growing out of the depredations of the *Alabama* and other Confederate cruisers fitted out in British ports

4   49

during the American civil war. The government of the United States, in demanding indemnities for these depredations, could point to the precedent of 1793; but in the case of the *Alabama* claims the amounts involved were enormous, and the British government besides denied that it had been guilty of any neglect. By the treaty of Washington, of May 8, 1871, the question was submitted to arbitration at Geneva. The treaty declared that a neutral government was bound to use "due diligence" in the performance of its duties. The tribunal found that there had been negligence on the part of the British authorities in respect of three of the cruisers —the *Alabama*, the *Florida*, and the *Shenandoah* after she left Melbourne—and awarded the United States $15,500,000. For the depredations of the French privateers in 1793 the United States paid to the subjects of Great Britain $143,428.11. The amount was relatively small, but its payment, on considerations of international obligation and good faith, established a principle incalculably important, and, like the seed received into good ground, brought forth a hundredfold, and even more.

It is perhaps not generally known that the *Alabama*, in spite of the omission of the English customs authorities to seize her, might in the end have been detained but for an act of wifely devotion. On the 22d and 24th of July, 1862, evidence directly inculpating the vessel was communicated by the Amer-

FACSIMILE OF COIN CERTIFICATE WITH WHICH THE GENEVA AWARD WAS PAID ican legation in London to the British Foreign Office. On the 23d and 26th of July the papers were referred to the law officers of the crown, and, as the law officers had no permanent office, were sent as usual to the senior officer, who was then Sir John Dorney Harding, Queen's Advocate, his associates being Sir William Atherton, Attorney-General, and Sir Roundell Palmer, afterwards Lord Selborne, Solicitor-General. Unfortunately, Sir John Harding had just then fallen a victim to an acute mental disorder, which proved to be fatal, but which his wife, in the hope that it would soon pass away, had kept a secret. Upon the decision to be rendered by the law officers there hung, perchance, the issues of peace and war and the fate of nations; but the papers lay unexamined at Sir John's residence apparently till the 28th of July, when the Foreign Office, growing anxious at the delay, but ignorant of its cause, took steps to recover them and placed them in the hands of Sir William Atherton. On the evening of the same day, Sir William, perceiving the gravity of the situation, which the papers disclosed, called Sir Roundell Palmer into consultation upon them in the Earl Marshal's room in the House of Lords. They at once agreed that the vessel must be seized. An opinion to that effect was delivered to Earl Russell on the morning of the 29th of July; but during the night of the 28th the *Alabama*, as if conscious of what was impending left the docks in which she had been lying. At ten o'clock on the morning of the 29th she put to sea. The order of the Foreign Office to detain her reached Liverpool in the afternoon.

The government of the United States, in 1793, had barely entered upon the performance of the duties of neutrality when it was swept into the vortex of the great struggle, which was to last almost unbroken for more than twenty years, for the maintenance of neutral rights. In this momentous contest there was involved the ever-recurrent question, which will continue in some form to arise as long as wars are waged, as to how far neutral powers are required to subordinate the interests of their commerce to the hostile interests of belligerents. That powers at peace were entitled to trade with powers at war was not denied, but the rule was subject to exceptions. It was admitted that a belligerent might cut off all trade with the enemy's ports by blockading them, and might also prohibit the carriage of contraband to the enemy. For entering or attempting to enter a blockaded port, the penalty was confiscation of vessel and cargo, while the carriage of contraband entailed the loss of the prohibited articles and the freight, if nothing more. There was, however, no precise and general agreement either as to what constituted a blockade, or as to what articles were to be considered as contraband. If blockades could be legally established merely by decrees on paper, without the application of force, or if the list of contraband could be sufficiently extended, it is obvious that the right of neutrals to trade with belligerents could be reduced to the shadow of a tantalizing supposition. Grotius, often called the father of international law, had divided articles, with reference to the question of contraband, into three classes: First, articles that were directly useful in war, as arms; second, those that were useless in war; and third, those that could be "used both in war and in peace, as money, provisions, ships, and articles of naval equipment." Concerning the first and second classes there was no dispute, except as to the possible inclusion or exclusion of some particular article; but as to the third class there had been a long and heated controversy, especially respecting provisions.

There was also a question as to whether the goods of an enemy might be seized on board a neutral ship. It was conceded that a belligerent power might capture vessels belonging to subjects of the enemy, as well as other private property of the enemy at sea; but for many years an effort had been in progress to introduce the rule, denoted by the phrase "free ships free goods," that the merchandise of an enemy should, unless contraband of war, be exempt from seizure when transported by a neutral vessel. In 1780, the Empress Catherine of Russia issued a famous declaration concerning neutral rights. Since the days when Peter the

Great, barbarian, statesman, and seer, diversified his studies in shipbuilding by riding through Evelyn's hedges in a wheelbarrow and pulling the teeth of his own retinue, Russia had aspired to become a maritime power. The declaration of the Empress Catherine afforded a striking manifestation of that ambition. Affirming the right of neutrals to trade with the powers at war, it sought to limit the scope of contraband, declared that blockades must be maintained by a force sufficient to render access to the blockaded port dangerous, and adopted the rule of free ships free goods. On this manifesto there was based an alliance of neutral powers, called the Armed Neutrality, the formation of which was one of the most notable events of the wars growing out of the American Revolution; and although the alliance was not effectively maintained, the principles which it consecrated possessed vitality, and were destined to survive an ordeal yet more severe than any to which they had ever been subjected.

By a decree of the National Convention of France, of May 9, 1793, the commanders of French ships of war and privateers were authorized to seize merchant vessels laden with provisions bound to an enemy's port, or with merchandise belonging to an enemy. This decree was defended on the ground of a scarcity of provisions in France, but it ran counter to the views of the United States concerning the freedom of trade as well as to treaty stipulations. Morris remonstrated against it, and intimated that it would be followed with eagerness by France's maritime enemies. His prognostication proved to be correct. By an order in council of June 8, 1793, the commanders of British cruisers were authorized to seize all vessels laden with grain, flour, or meal, bound either to a port in France or to a port occupied by the French arms. It is true that, by the terms of both these measures, the provisions, if neutral-owned, were to be paid for; but the compensation promised was far less than the cargo would have brought at the port of destination. Moreover, the order in council was followed, as was also the decree, by other measures yet more vexatious.

Out of these perilous complications Washington sought to find a way by negotiation. John Jay, then Chief-Justice of the United States, was sent to London, where, on November 19, 1794, he concluded a treaty under which an aggregate amount of perhaps more than eleven million dollars was eventually obtained from the British government on account of maritime captures. The treaty, however, gave great umbrage to France, not only because it granted privileges of asylum to British ships of war and recognized the right to capture enemies' goods in neutral vessels, but also because it definitely fixed the position of the United States as a neutral. The resentment of the French government was soon made

JOHN JAY

manifest by measures which prefigured the Berlin and Milan decrees of Napoleon. By a decree of the Executive Directory of July 2, 1796, which laid the foundation of a new series, it was announced that the cruisers of France would treat neutral vessels, as to searches, captures, and confiscation, in the same manner as their governments should suffer the English to treat them. The French government also recalled its minister from the United States and reduced the grade of the mission. Monroe, too, was recalled, and in his place was sent Charles Cotesworth Pinckney.

When, in December, 1796, Pinckney arrived in Paris, the Directory refused either to receive him or to permit him to stay at the capital as a private alien; and he retired to Amsterdam to await developments. Desirous, however, of trying all possible means of conciliation, President John Adams, while recommending to Congress the consideration of effectual measures of defence, joined Elbridge Gerry and John Marshall with Pinckney in a special mission. The three envoys arrived in Paris October 4, 1797. Four days later they were unofficially received by Talleyrand, who was then Minister of Foreign Affairs; but he subsequently intimated that they could not have a public audience of the Directory till their negotiations were concluded. Meanwhile, they were waited upon by three men who came sometimes singly and sometimes together, and who professed to represent Talleyrand and the Directory. These persons are known in the correspondence as X, Y, and Z. Their approach was prepared by W, who called on Pinckney and vouched for X as a gentleman of credit and reputation, in whom great reliance might be placed. On the evening of the same day X called, and, professing to speak for Talleyrand, suggested confidentially a plan of conciliation. He represented that certain passages in President Adams's recent speech to Congress, at which two members of the Directory were exceedingly irritated, would need to be softened; that a sum of money, to be at the disposal of Talleyrand, would be required as a *douceur* for the ministry, except Merlin, the Minister of Justice, who was already making enough from the condemnation of vessels; and that a loan to the government would also be insisted on. X stated, however, that he communicated with Talleyrand not directly, but through another gentleman, in whom Talleyrand had great confidence. This gentleman proved to be Y, who afterwards called with X upon the American plenipotentiaries and presented the propositions in writing. Y also dilated upon the resentment produced by the President's speech, but declared that, after the plenipotentiaries had afforded satisfaction on that point, they must pay money, "a great deal of money." In so saying he referred to the subject of a loan. Concerning the *douceur* little was said, it

being understood that it was required for the officers of government, and therefore needed no further
explanation. An impression perhaps widely pre-
vails that at this point Pinckney exclaimed, "Millions for defence, but not a cent for tribute," and
·broke off the negotiations. The story is a pretty
one, but is inaccurate. The sentiment in question,
which resembles a phrase used by Jefferson, when
Secretary of State, in his correspondence with the
Barbary powers, was pronounced as a toast at a
public dinner given to Marshall, at Philadelphia, on
his return from France. In reality, the American
plenipotentiaries, although they repulsed the solicita-
tions of personal venality with the reply, "No, no,
not a sixpence," offered to consult their government with regard to a loan, if the Directory would
suspend its measures against American commerce.
This the Directory refused to do. Negotiations
were ended; the treaties between the two countries
were abrogated by the United States; and there
succeeded the state of limited war which prevailed
from 1798 till 1800.

The respite which commerce enjoyed from belligerent depredations after the Peace of Amiens was
of brief duration, and the renewal of war, in 1803,
was ere long followed by measures which retain in
the history of belligerent pretensions an unhappy
pre-eminence. The "rule of the War of 1756," by
which Great Britain had assumed to forbid neutrals

to engage during war in a trade from which they were excluded in time of peace, was enforced by the British admiralty courts with new stringency under cover of the doctrine of continuous voyages. Moreover, the British government in 1806, in retaliation for a decree of Prussia, which was issued under Napoleonic compulsion, excluding British trade from that country, declared the mouths of the Ems, the Weser, the Elbe, and the Trave to be in a state of blockade. On November 21, 1806, Napoleon fulminated from the imperial camp at Berlin a decree declaring the British Islands to be in a state of blockade and prohibiting all commerce and correspondence with them. Great Britain replied by an order in council of January 6, 1807, forbidding neutral vessels to trade between ports in the control of France or her allies; and by still another order, November 11, 1807, she forbade such vessels to trade with the ports of France and her allies, or even with any port in Europe from which the British flag was excluded, without a clearance obtained in a British port. Napoleon's answer was the Milan decree of December 17, 1807, by which it was declared that every vessel that had submitted to search by an English ship, or consented to a voyage to England, or paid any tax to the English government, as well as every vessel that should sail to or from a port in Great Britain or her possessions, or in any country occupied by British troops, should be deemed good prize.

These measures, with their bald assertions of paper blockades and sweeping denials of the rights of neutrality, the United States, as practically the only remaining neutral, met with protests, with embargoes, with non-intercourse, and finally, in the case of Great Britain, which was aggravated by the question of impressment, to which President Madison gave so much prominence in his war message, with hostile resistance, while from France a considerable indemnity was afterwards obtained by treaty. The pretensions against which the United States contended are no longer justified on legal grounds. Since the Declaration of Paris of 1856, it has been universally admitted that a blockade, in order to be valid, must be effective. The right of neutrals to trade with belligerents is acknowledged, subject only to the law of contraband and of blockade.

There is one radical limitation to belligerent activities, which, although often urged, has not yet been adopted. This is the inhibition of the capture of private property at sea. Strongly advocated by Franklin, it was introduced into the first treaty between the United States and Prussia, in the signature of which he was associated with Adams and Jefferson. John Quincy Adams, Henry Clay, William L. Marcy, and Hamilton Fish are among the great Secretaries of State who have given the principle their support. President McKinley, in his annual message of December 5, 1898, suggested to Congress that the Executive be authorized to correspond with the governments of the principal maritime powers of the world with a view to incorporate it into the permanent law of civilized nations. This recommendation is cordially renewed by President Roosevelt in his annual message of December 7, 1903, in which the exemption, except as to contraband of war, is advocated not only as a matter of "humanity and morals," but also as a measure altogether compatible with the practical conduct of war at sea.

III

IN maintaining the right of neutrals freely to navigate the ocean in pursuit of innocent commerce, the early statesmen of America, while sustaining a predominant national interest, gave their support to a cause from the eventual triumph of which the whole world was to derive an incalculable benefit. But it was not in time of war alone that commerce was exposed to attacks at sea. Although the exorbitant pretensions of the sixteenth century, by which the navigation even of the Atlantic and the Pacific was assumed to be susceptible of engrossment, had, before the end of the eighteenth, fallen into desuetude, much remained to be accomplished before the exhibition of an acknowledged national flag would assure to the peaceful mariner an unmolested passage. Ere this great end could be attained, it was necessary that various exaggerated claims of dominion over adjacent seas should be denied and overcome, that the "right of search" should be resisted and abandoned, and that piracy should be extirpated.

In placing the danger from "water thieves" before the peril of "waters, winds, and rocks," Shylock described a condition of things that long survived his own times. At the close of the eighteenth century, a merchantman built for long voyages still differed little in armament from a man-of-war. Whether it rounded the Horn or the Cape of Good Hope, it was exposed to the depredations of ferocious and well-armed marauders, and if it passed through the Straits of Gibraltar it was forced to encounter maritime blackmail in its most systematic and most authoritative form. On the African coast of the Mediterranean lay the Barbary powers—the empire of Morocco, and the regencies of Tunis, Tripoli, and Algiers—which had for generations subsisted by depredations on commerce. In this way they had won the opprobrious title of "piratical states," but they wore it with a pampered and supercilious dignity. Even in the exchange of courtesies they exhibited a haughty parsimony, exacting from the foreign man-of-war the generous requital of a barrel of powder for every gun with which they returned its salute. They had every reason to know that their power was understood and dreaded. In their navies might be found the products of the ship-building skill of England, France, Spain, and Venice. In war, civilized powers did not always scruple to make use of their aid. Their mode of life was diplomatically recognized, and to some extent connived at. It was regulated by a simple formula. While disdaining the part of common pirates, such as plundered vessels indiscriminately, they professed themselves at war with all who refused to pay them tribute; and they took good care to make their friendship expensive. Peace with Algiers, in 1786, was reported to have cost Spain upward of three millions of dollars, while the annual presents of Great Britain to the four states were valued at nearly three hundred thousand.

At the outbreak of the Revolution it was estimated that one-sixth of the wheat and flour exported from the United States, and one-fourth of their dried and pickled fish, and a quantity of rice, found their best market in the ports of the Mediterranean. In this commerce, which had grown up under the protection of the British flag, there were employed from eighty to a hundred ships, manned by twelve hundred seamen. Early in the war it was entirely abandoned, and its loss was severely felt. In the plan of a treaty furnished to Franklin and his colleagues, the Continental Congress, accommodating its demands to its wishes, proposed that France should take the place of Great Britain as the protector of American vessels; but the King of France went no further than to agree to lend his good offices. During the Revolution the Mediterranean commerce therefore remained in abeyance; but on May 12, 1784, Adams, Franklin, and Jefferson were commissioned to treat with the Barbary powers; and on the 11th of the ensuing March they were authorized to send agents to those countries to negotiate. The government acted none too soon. Before an agent was appointed to Morocco, an American vessel was captured by a cruiser of that state. The Emperor, however, exhibited much mildness. On the friendly interposition of Spain, he restored the vessel and cargo and released the crew; and in January, 1787, he concluded a liberal treaty, at a cost to the United States of less than ten thousand dollars.

The other powers proved to be less tractable, and especially troublesome was the Dey of Algiers, by whose activities the revival of American commerce with the Mediterranean was for a time effectually prevented. On July 25, 1785, the schooner *Maria*, of Boston, was captured off Cape St. Vincent by an Algerine cruiser, and five days later the ship *Dauphin*, of Philadelphia, was taken. The vessels and their cargoes were carried to Algiers, and all on board, embracing twenty-one persons, were, according to custom, consigned to slavery till they should be ransomed. A new difficulty was thus created. When Congress issued its commission to Adams and his associates, there were thousands of captives in Barbary; but, as there were no Americans among them, the question of ransom was not considered, and the whole expense of the negotiations was

limited to eighty thousand dollars. For the liberation of the twenty - one Americans subsequently
captured, Algiers demanded two - thirds of that
sum. For this emergency no provision had been
made. When the new government under the Constitution was formed, Jefferson, as Secretary of
State, declared the determination of the United
States "to prefer war, in all cases, to tribute under
any form," but a navy was wanting to make
this declaration effective. By December, 1793,
the number of American vessels captured by Algerine corsairs had risen to thirteen, and the number of captives to a hundred and nineteen. From
Boston to Norfolk almost every seaport had furnished its victim. Nor was the Dey anxious to
make peace with America. So successful had he
been in bringing other governments to terms, that
he remained at war only with the United States and
the Hanse Towns, and he began to grow apprehen-
sive at the prospect of inactivity. "If," he exclaimed, "I were to make peace with everybody,
what should I do with my corsairs? What should
I do with my soldiers? They would take off my
head for the want of other prizes, not being able to
live upon their miserable allowance." Reasoning
thus, he was not disposed to compromise; but the
government of the United States, urged on by the
cry of the captives, whom it was then unable to
rescue by force, accepted his conditions, and, by

the expenditure of nearly eight hundred thousand dollars, obtained the release of its citizens and purchased a peace, which was signed on September 5, 1795. A treaty with Tripoli followed on November 4, 1796, and with Tunis in August, 1797.

The respite thus secured was of brief duration. The Dey of Algiers received, under his treaty with the United States, an annual payment of twelve thousand sequins (equivalent to nearly twenty-two thousand dollars) in naval stores, but, besides this stipulated tribute, there were customary payments that were rigorously counted as regalian rights. Among these were included a present of twenty thousand dollars on the sending out of a new consul, biennial presents to officers of government estimated at seventeen thousand dollars, and incidental and contingent presents of which no forecast could be made. Tribute was likewise paid to Tripoli and to Tunis; but the potentates of the regencies, though they pursued a common interest, were jealous of one another's prosperity in peace as well as in war, and were hard to content. Early in 1800 the Bashaw of Tripoli, Jusuf Caramanly, a bold usurper who seems to have understood both the principles and the cant of thrifty politics, complained to Mr. Cathcart, the American consul, that the presents of the United States to Algiers and Tunis were more liberal than those to himself; and he significantly added that compliments, although acceptable, were of little account, and that the heads of the Barbary states knew their friends by the value of the presents they received from them. Not long afterwards he intimated that he would like to have some American captives to teach him English, and that, if the United States flag once came down, it would take a great deal of "grease" to raise it again. Finally, lest the seriousness of his grievances might not be appreciated, he addressed himself directly to the President, to whom he pointedly declared that any delay in complying with his demands would be prejudicial to American interests. No response came, and the Bashaw grew impatient. "In Tripoli, consul," said he, to Cathcart, "we are all hungry, and if we are not provided for we soon get sick and peevish." Cathcart, seeing that the Bashaw spoke in metaphors, replied that, when the chief physician prescribed the medicine, he should not object to administering it, but that meanwhile he could promise nothing. "Take care," answered the Bashaw, "that the medicine does not come too late, and, if it comes in time, that it is strong enough." On May 14, 1801, he caused the American flag-staff to be chopped down six feet from the ground, in token of war. The answer of the United States had already been decided upon. Symptoms of unrest had appeared in Tunis and Algiers as well as in Tripoli; and a squadron was sent to the Mediterranean with orders, if any of the Barbary powers should declare war or commit hostilities, to protect American commerce and chastise their insolence. The government had, as President Jefferson declared, determined "to owe to our own energies, and not to dishonorable condescensions, the protection of our right to navigate the ocean freely." For two years the contest with Tripoli dragged wearily along, but its vigorous prosecution with augmented forces, after the summer of 1803, brought it at length to a triumphant close. The midnight destruction by Decatur of the frigate *Philadelphia*, under the fire of the Bashaw's gunboats and batteries; the fierce and incessant bombardments by Preble of the Tripolitan stronghold; the mysterious fate of the heroic Somers and his fire-ship; and the intrepid march of Eaton across the desert to the capture of Derne, were incidents which taught the rulers of the Barbary coast that a new spirit must be reckoned with. On June 3, 1805, peace was agreed to by a representative of the Bashaw on board the frigate *Constitution*, and next day a treaty was concluded on shore.

During the seven years that followed the second peace with Tripoli, the relations of the United States with the Barbary powers were comparatively uneventful; but their tranquillity was now and then disturbed by incidents which, although they did not produce a rupture, bespoke a sullen dissatisfaction with existing conditions. This feeling prompt-

ly flamed out when in 1812 the report was received
of war between the United States and Great Britain.
The Dey of Algiers, encouraged to believe that the
maritime power of America would be annihilated,
discovered that the United States had always fallen
short in the payment of tribute, and expelled the
American consul-general and all American citizens
from his dominions. An American brig was captured by an Algerine corsair, and the crew reduced
to captivity, while an American passenger was taken
out of a Spanish ship and held in bondage. Tripoli
and Tunis allowed the prizes of an American priva-
teer to be recaptured by the British in their ports.
As the war with England had practically shut the
Mediterranean against American vessels, measures
of defence were deferred; but on February 23, 1815,
five days after peace with Great Britain was proclaimed, President Madison recommended a declaration of war against Algiers. The response of
Congress was at once made in an act, approved on
March 3d, "for the protection of the commerce of
the United States against the Algerine cruisers."
Two squadrons were ordered to the Mediterranean,
under Bainbridge and Decatur. Decatur, arriving
first on the scene, compelled the Dey on June 30th
to agree to a treaty by which it was declared that
no tribute, under any name or form whatsoever,
should again be required from the United States.
No other nation had ever obtained such terms.

Tripoli and Tunis were also duly admonished; and the passage of the Straits of Gibraltar was relieved of its burdens and its terrors.

With the suppression of the Barbary exactions, tolerated piracy disappeared; but the depredations of lawless freebooters in various parts of the world long continued to furnish occasion for naval and to some extent for diplomatic activity. As late as 1870 the naval forces of the United States were directed, upon the invitation of Prussia, to co-operate with those of the other powers for the suppression of piracy in Chinese waters. Such incidents, however, possess no special significance. No one undertakes to defend confessed lawlessness. Attempts to abridge the freedom of the seas assume a dangerous form, and become important when they are made or sanctioned by governments, on pleas of pretended right or interest. Within this category fell the claim long strenuously asserted that the cruisers of one nation might lawfully visit and search the merchant vessels of another nation on the high seas, in peace as well as in war. To the people of the United States this claim was rendered especially hateful by the practice of impressment, with which it came to be peculiarly identified. From time immemorial the commanders of men-of-war had been in the habit, when searching neutral vessels for contraband or enemy's property, of taking out and pressing into service any seamen whom they conceived to be their fellow-subjects. The practice was essentially irregular, arbitrary, and oppressive, but its most mischievous possibilities were yet to be developed in the conditions resulting from American independence. After Great Britain, in 1793, became involved in the wars growing out of the French Revolution, the nature and extent of those possibilities were soon disclosed. Not only were the native sailors of England and America generally indistinguishable by the obvious test of language, but the crews of American vessels often contained a large proportion of men of British birth, who, even when naturalized in the United States, were, under the doctrine of indelible allegiance then almost universally prevalent, still claimed by Great Britain as her subjects. Native Americans, if mistakenly impressed, ran the risk of being killed in action before an order could be obtained for their release; all others were firmly held to service. Nor was it a slight inconvenience that in this way American crews were sometimes so far depleted as to be unable to navigate their ships. The United States, while freely admitting the belligerent right of search, denied that it might be employed for any but the acknowledged purposes of enforcing blockades, seizing prize goods, and perhaps capturing officers and soldiers in the actual service of the enemy. "The simplest rule," declared Jefferson, when Secretary of State, "will be that the vessel being American shall be evidence that the seamen on board are such." Efforts were repeatedly made by the United States to adjust the controversy, but in vain. President Madison gave it the chief place in his message of June 1, 1812, recommending war against Great Britain; but in the treaty of peace concluded at Ghent, December 24, 1814, it was not mentioned. Nearly thirty years later, Webster, when Secretary of State, recurring to Jefferson's rule, declared: "In every regularly documented American merchant-vessel the crew who navigate it will find their protection in the flag which is over them." These words were addressed to Lord Ashburton on August 8, 1842. The principle of protection and immunity which they announced was asserted in even broader terms, and was thus impliedly accepted by the British government in 1861. On November 8th in that year the British mail-steamer *Trent*, while on a voyage from Havana to St. Thomas, was overhauled by the American man-of-war *San Jacinto*, Captain Wilkes, and was compelled to surrender the Confederate commissioners Messrs. Mason and Slidell, and their secretaries, Messrs. McFarland and Eustis, all of whom were on their way to England. The sole reason given by Earl Russell for demanding their release was that "certain individuals" had "been forcibly taken from on board a British vessel, the ship of a neutral power, while such vessel was pursuing a lawful and innocent voyage—an act of violence which was an affront to the British flag and a violation of international law." No wonder that Mr. Seward, in assuring Lord Lyons that the demand would be granted, congratulated himself on defending and maintaining "an old, honored, and cherished American cause."

The controversy as to impressment involved no question as to search on the high seas in time of peace. Such a right had been asserted by Spain and other powers for the purpose of enforcing their colonial restrictions. The United States refused to admit it, and conceded a right of search in time of peace only in respect of pirates, who, as enemies of the human race, were held to be outside the pale of national protection. Beyond this the government refused to go. As the war-right of search had been perverted to the purpose of impressment, so it was apprehended that the peace-right, if any were admitted to exist, might be perverted to the same purpose or to purposes equally odious.

To this position the United States tenaciously adhered, even when strongly solicited to depart from it by the promptings of philanthropy. The movement so energetically led by Great Britain during the first half of the nineteenth century, for the suppression of the African slave-trade, found in all civilized lands strong support in public opinion. To its success, however, the voluntary co-operation of nations was discovered to be indispensable. Soon after the close of the Napoleonic wars, Lord Stowell, the greatest judge that ever sat in the English Court of Admiralty, declared in the case of a French vessel, which had been seized by a British cruiser on a charge of engaging in the slave-trade, that no nation could exercise a right of visitation and search upon the common and unappropriated part of the ocean except from belligerent claim. The vessel was discharged. As if to anticipate such an obstacle, the British government had already entered into treaties with Denmark, Portugal, and Spain, by which a qualified right of search was conceded; and it sought to make the measure universal. So steadfastly was the object pursued that by 1850 the number of such treaties in force between Great Britain and other powers was twenty - four. Among the assenting governments, however, the two most important powers were not found — the United States and France. When the proposal was submitted to the United States, the government at once repulsed it. No man condemned the slave-trade more strongly than did John Quincy Adams; on the other hand, no one more profoundly appreciated the fundamental principles of American policy and the importance of maintaining them. In 1818, when Secretary of State, he declared that the admission of the right of search in time of peace, under any circumstances whatever, would meet with universal repugnance in the United States. He steadily re-

JOHN QUINCY ADAMS

sisted in Monroe's cabinet, even in opposition to the yielding inclinations of Calhoun and other members from slave States, any abatement of this position. The subject was, however, taken up in Congress, and by an act of May 15, 1820, the slave-trade was branded as piracy. This act seemed to constitute the first step on the part of the United States towards the assimilation of the traffic, by the consent of the civilized world, to piracy by law of nations, thus bringing it within the operation of the only acknowledged right of search in time of peace; and by a resolution of the House of Representatives, passed on February 28, 1823, by a vote of 131 to 9, the President was requested to open negotiations to that end. Instructions in conformity with this resolution were given to the diplomatic representatives of the United States; and on March 13, 1824, a convention was signed at London which conceded a reciprocal right of search on the coasts of Africa, America, and the West Indies. The Senate of the United States, however, on May 21, 1824, by a vote of 36 to 2, struck out the word "America," and, the British government declining to accept the amendment, the treaty failed. On December 10, 1824, the Senate rejected a similar convention with Colombia, although it did not apply to the American coasts. Negotiations on the subject were therefore discontinued, and the decision not to concede even a qualified right of search was adhered to.

The government of the United States was not insensible to the crying evils of the traffic in slaves. In the treaty of Ghent, it had concurred in reprobating the traffic as "irreconcilable with the principles of humanity and justice," and had pledged its best endeavors to accomplish its entire abolition. But, while always acknowledging, as it did in the Webster-Asburton treaty, the duty to employ its naval forces for the redemption of that pledge, it insisted that American vessels on the high seas should be liable to search only by American cruisers; and it conceded a similar exemption to the vessels of other nations. In 1858 this principle was at length formally accepted by the British government; and in the same year the Senate of the United States unanimously reaffirmed it. Since that time, the United States has in three instances consented to a qualified departure from its observance: in the treaties with Great Britain, concluded April 7, 1862, and February 17, 1863, during the civil war, admitting a reciprocal search for slavers within two hundred miles from the African coast southward of the thirty-second parallel of north latitude, and within thirty leagues of the islands of Cuba, Puerto Rico, Santo Domingo, and Madagascar; in the general act of Brussels of July 2, 1890, permitting, for the purpose of repressing the slave-trade, a mutual search within a defined zone on the eastern coast of Africa of vessels of less than five hundred tons bur-

den; and in the agreements for the protection of
the fur seals in Bering Sea. By the abolition of
slavery in the Spanish Antilles, the most doubtful
concession made in the treaties with Great Britain
soon ceased practically to cause anxiety; nor was
the integrity of the general principle impaired by
the exceptional and temporary relaxation of its
observance by mutual agreement. It may indeed
be said that the making of such agreements by the
United States was rendered possible by the previous
unqualified acceptance of the principle of the freedom of the seas by Great Britain and other maritime powers.

The disposition of the United States to maintain
its general and time-honored rule was signally exemplified in the case of the steamer *Virginius*. On
October 31, 1873, the *Virginius*, while sailing under
an American register and flying the American flag,
was chased and seized on the high seas off the
coast of Cuba by the Spanish man-of-war *Tornado*.
The captive vessel was taken to Santiago de Cuba,
where, after a summary trial by court - martial,
ostensibly on a charge of piracy, fifty-three of her
officers, crew, and passengers, embracing Americans,
British subjects, and Cubans, were condemned and
shot. The rest were held as prisoners. No foundation was shown for the charge of piracy beyond the
fact that the vessel was employed by Cuban insurgents in conveying arms, ammunition, and men to

Cuba, an employment which obviously did not constitute piracy by law of nations. The government of the United States therefore demanded the restoration of the vessel, the surrender of the captives, a salute to the American flag, and the condign punishment of the Spanish officials. On proof that the register of the *Virginius* was fraudulent, and that she had no right to American colors, the salute to the flag was afterwards dispensed with; but the vessel and the survivors of her passengers and crew were duly delivered up; and an indemnity was eventually obtained by the United States for the relief of the sufferers and of the families of those who were put to death, with the exception of the British subjects, for whom compensation was obtained from Spain by their own government. It is often stated that the United States in this case maintained that the *Virginius* was exempt from search merely because she bore the American flag, even though her papers were false and she had no right to fly it. This supposition is contradicted by the fact that the salute to the flag was dispensed with. The demands of the United States in their last analysis rested chiefly upon the ground that the vessel was unlawfully seized on a spurious charge of piracy, and that the proceedings at Santiago de Cuba were conducted in flagrant disregard of law and of the treaties between the two countries. In March, 1895, the American steamer, *Alliança*, bound from Colon to New York, was fired on by a Spanish gunboat off the coast of Cuba outside the three-mile limit. The Spanish government promptly disavowed the act and expressed regret, and, by way of assurance that such an event would not again occur, relieved the offending officer of his command. Incidents such as these serve to show that the principle of the freedom of the seas has lost neither its vitality nor its importance. It may indeed be said that the exemption of vessels from visitation and search on the high seas in time of peace is a principle which rather grows than diminishes in the estimation of mankind; for in the light of history, its establishment is seen to mark the progress of commerce from a semi-barbarous condition, in which it was exposed to constant violence, to its present state of freedom and security. Nor is there any page in American diplomacy more glorious than that on which the successful advocacy of this great principle is recorded.

While maintaining the freedom of the seas, the United States has also contended for the free navigation of the natural channels by which they are connected. On this principle, it led in the movement that brought about the abolition, in 1857, of the dues levied by Denmark on vessels and cargoes passing through the sound and belts which form a passage from the North Sea into the Baltic. These dues, which were justified by the Danish government on the ground of immemorial usage, sanctioned by a long succession of treaties, and of the benefit conferred on shipping by the policing and lighting of the waters, bore heavily on commerce, and the United States, after repeatedly remonstrating, at length gave notice that it would no longer submit to them. This action led to the calling of a conference in Europe. The United States declined to take part in it, but afterwards co-operated, by a treaty with Denmark, in giving effect to the plan under which the dues were capitalized and removed. An artificial channel necessarily involves special consideration; but, reasoning by analogy, Mr. Clay, as Secretary of State, declared that if a canal to unite the Pacific and Atlantic oceans should ever be constructed, "the benefits of it ought not to be exclusively appropriated to any one nation, but should be extended to all parts of the globe upon the payment of a just compensation or reasonable tolls." This principle was approved by the Senate in 1835, and by the House of Representatives in 1839, and was incorporated in the Clayton-Bulwer treaty in 1850. It is now embodied in the Hay-Pauncefote treaty for the neutralization of the interoceanic canal.

Nor should we omit to mention, in connection with the freedom of the seas, the subject of the free navigation of international rivers. It is not doubted that rivers such as the Hudson and the Mississippi, which are navigable only within the territory of one country, are subject to that country's exclusive control. But with regard to rivers which are navigable within two or more countries, the principle of free navigation, consecrated in the acts of the Congress of Vienna, has been consistently advocated by the United States, and has been embodied in various forms in several of its treaties. When the British government sought to deny to the inhabitants of the United States the commercial use of the river St. Lawrence, Henry Clay, as Secretary of State, appealed to the regulations of the Congress of Vienna, which should, he declared, "be regarded only as the spontaneous homage of man to the superior wisdom of the paramount Lawgiver of the Universe, by delivering His great works from the artificial shackles and selfish contrivances to which they have been arbitrarily and unjustly subjected." The free navigation of the St. Lawrence was secured temporarily by the reciprocity treaty of 1854, and in perpetuity by the treaty of Washington of 1871, which also declared the rivers, Yukon, Porcupine, and Stikine to be "forever free and open for purposes of commerce" to the citizens of both countries. For many years the government of the United States actively endeavored to secure the free navigation of the Amazon, which was at length voluntarily conceded by the Emperor of Brazil to all nations in 1866. By a treaty between the United States and

83

Bolivia of 1858, the Amazon and La Plata, with their tributaries, were declared to be, "in accordance with fixed principles of international law, . . . channels open by nature for the commerce of all nations." In 1852, General Urquiza, provisional director of the Argentine Confederation, decreed that the navigation of the rivers Parana and Uruguay should be open to the vessels of all nations. In the next year the United States, acting concurrently with France and Great Britain, secured the confirmation of this privilege by treaty. The State of Buenos Ayres, which had sought to control the commercial possibilities which the rivers afforded, protested against the treaties and withdrew from the confederation; but the treaty powers decided to bestow the moral weight and influence of diplomatic relations upon the government which had been prompt to recognize the liberal commercial principles of the age, and the policy of free navigation prevailed.

From Paraguay, which had sought to lead the life of a hermit state, a similar concession was obtained under peculiar circumstances. In 1853 the government of the United States sent out a naval vessel, called the *Water Witch*, under the command of Lieutenant Thomas J. Page, to survey the tributaries of the river Plate and report on the commercial condition of the countries bordering on their waters. Permission was obtained from the government of Brazil to explore all the waters of the Paraguay that were under Brazilian jurisdiction, and from the provisional director of the Argentine Confederation to explore all rivers within the jurisdiction of his government. The surveys of the Plate, and of the Paraguay and the Parana, had been in progress about a year and a half, when, on January 31, 1855, Lieutenant Page started from Corrientes with a small steamer and two boats to ascend the river Salado, leaving Lieutenant William N. Jeffers in charge of the *Water Witch*, with instructions to ascend the Parana as far as her draught would allow. Lieutenant Jeffers sailed from Corrientes on the 1st of February, and had proceeded only a few miles above the point where the Parana forms the common boundary between Paraguay and the Argentine province of Corrientes, when he ran aground near the Paraguayan fort of Itapiru. An hour later the *Water Witch* was hauled off and anchored; but while the crew were at dinner it was observed that the Paraguayans were getting their guns ready. Lieutenant Jeffers, though not expecting serious trouble, had the *Water Witch* cleared for action and gave directions to proceed up the river at all hazards. While he was weighing anchor, a Paraguayan canoe came alongside and a man on board handed him a paper in Spanish. This paper Jeffers declined to receive, since he did not understand the language in which it was printed, and as

85

soon as the anchor was raised he stood up the river, the crew at quarters. The pilot informed him that the only practicable channel lay close to the fort, on the Paraguayan side of the river, and this he directed the pilot to take. When within three hundred yards from the fort he was hailed, presumably in Spanish, by a person who was said to be the Paraguayan admiral, but not understanding the import of the hail he did not regard it. Two blank cartridges were then fired by the fort in quick succession, and these were followed by a shot which carried away the wheel of the *Water Witch*, cut the ropes, and mortally wounded the helmsman. Lieutenant Jeffers directed a general fire in return, and the action continued for some minutes. In 1858, the government of the United States sent an expedition to Paraguay to obtain reparation for this and other incidents. The American minister, who accompanied the fleet, obtained "ample apologies," as well as an indemnity of $10,000 for the family of the seaman who was killed at the wheel; and on February 4, 1859, a treaty of amity and commerce was concluded at Asuncion, by which Paraguay conceded "to the merchant flag of the citizens of the United States" the free navigation of the rivers Paraguay and Parana, so far as they lay within her dominions.

IV

FISHERIES QUESTIONS

As the cause of the freedom of the seas advanced, inordinate claims of dominion over adjacent waters naturally shrank and dwindled away. This tendency towards humaner opinions and practices may be traced in the history of fisheries questions. For more than three centuries, Denmark claimed the right, on grounds of sovereignty and dominion, to monopolize the fisheries in all the seas lying between Norway and Iceland. This claim, though eventually resisted by other powers, was acquiesced in by England by treaties made in 1400 and 1523, under which her merchants and fishermen plying their trade in those seas were required to take out licenses from the Danish King. At a later day the Dutch obtained licenses from the British government for the purpose of fishing in the North Sea. These examples serve to illustrate the practices that prevailed in times when exclusive rights were asserted not only as to fishing in gulfs and bays and in vast reaches of the open sea, but also as to particular fisheries, such as those on the Grand Banks of Newfoundland.

We have seen that among the subjects discussed by the peace commissioners of Great Britain and the United States at Paris in 1782, the two that were the most strongly contested and the last disposed of were those of the fisheries and the compensation of the loyalists. The provisional articles of peace were concluded November 30, 1782. On the 25th of that month the British commissioners delivered to the American commissioners a set of articles, containing fresh proposals from the British ministry, and representing the results of many weeks of negotiation. By these articles, the third of which related to the fisheries, the citizens of the United States were forbidden not only to dry fish on the shores of Nova Scotia, but also to take fish within three leagues of the coasts in the Gulf of St. Lawrence, and within fifteen leagues of the coasts of Cape Breton outside of that gulf. This proposal was unacceptable to the American commissioners; and on the 28th of November, John Adams drew up a counter-project, which was submitted in a conference of the commissioners on the following day. It provided that the subjects of his Britannic Majesty and the people of the United States should "continue to enjoy, unmolested, the right to take fish of every kind, on the Grand Bank, and on all the other banks of Newfoundland; also in the Gulf of St. Lawrence, and in all other places, where the inhabitants of both countries used at any time heretofore to fish"; and that the citizens of the United States should "have liberty to cure and dry their fish on the shores of Cape Sables, and any of the unsettled bays, harbors, or creeks of Nova Scotia, or any of the shores of the Magdalen Islands, and of the Labrador coast"; and that they should be "permitted, in time of peace, to hire pieces of land, for terms of years, of the legal proprietors, in any of the dominions of his Majesty, whereon to erect the necessary stages and buildings, and to cure and dry their fish." One of the British commissioners objected to the use of the word *right*, in respect of the taking of fish on the Grand Bank and other banks of Newfoundland, in the Gulf of St. Lawrence, "and in all other places, where the inhabitants of both countries used at any time heretofore to fish." Another said that "the word *right* was an obnoxious expression." Adams vehemently contended for the right of the people of America to fish on the banks of Newfoundland. "Can there be a clearer right?" he exclaimed. "In former treaties, that of Utrecht, and that of Paris, France and England claimed the right and have used the word." Finally, when he declared that he would not sign any articles without satisfaction in respect of the fishery, the British commissioners conceded the point, and after many suggestions and amendments a stipulation was agreed on which formed the third article of the provisional peace. By this article, which was based on the proposal submitted by Adams, it was agreed that the people of the United States should continue to enjoy the "right" to take fish on all the banks of Newfoundland and in the Gulf of St. Lawrence, and "at all other places in the sea" where the inhabitants of both countries had been accustomed to fish; and that the inhabitants of the United States should have the "liberty" to take fish on the coast of Newfoundland and on the coasts, bays, and creeks of all other of his Britannic Majesty's dominions in America, and also the "liberty" to dry and cure fish, subject to an agreement with the proprietors of the ground, so soon as any of the coasts should become settled.

When the representatives of the two countries met at Ghent, on August 8, 1814, to negotiate a new treaty of peace, the British plenipotentiaries at once took the ground that the fishery arrangement of 1782–83 had been terminated by the war of 1812, and declared that, while they "did not deny the right of the Americans to fish generally, or in the open seas," they could not renew the privilege of fishing within British jurisdiction and of drying fish on the British shores without an equivalent. In the discussions that ensued, the question of the free navigation of the Mississippi, which had been secured to British subjects by the treaty of 1782–83, became coupled with that of the fisheries. The American plenipotentiaries were unwilling to renew the stipulation as to the Mississippi; the British plenipotentiaries refused to yield the fisheries without it; and in the end, on motion of the Americans, a treaty of peace was concluded which contained no mention either of the fisheries or of the Mississippi. Both subjects were left for future negotiation.

On June 19, 1815, an American fishing-vessel, engaged in the cod-fishery, was, when about forty-five miles from Cape Sable, warned by the commander of the British sloop *Jaseur* not to come within sixty miles of the coast. This act the British government disavowed; but Lord Bathurst is reported at the same time to have declared that, while it was not the government's intention to interrupt American fishermen "in fishing anywhere in the open sea, or without the territorial jurisdiction, a marine league from the shore," it "could not permit the vessels of the United States to fish within the creeks and close upon the shores of the British territories." John Quincy Adams, who was then minister of the United States in London, maintained that the treaty of peace of 1783 "was not, in its general provisions, one of those which, by the common understanding and usage of civilized nations, is or can be considered as annulled by a subsequent war between the same parties." This position Lord Bathurst denied. He contended that the treaty of 1782–83, like many others, contained provisions of different characters— some irrevocable, and others of a temporary nature, terminable by war; and that the two governments had, in respect of the fisheries, recognized this distinction by describing as a "right" the open sea fishery, which the United States could enjoy merely by virtue of its independence, and as a "liberty," dependent on the treaty itself, what was to be done within British jurisdiction. This position the British government continued to maintain. From 1815 to 1818 many American vessels found fishing in British waters were seized, and much ill feeling was engendered.

Such was the condition of things when, on October 20, 1818, Albert Gallatin and Richard Rush concluded with plenipotentiaries on the part of Great Britain a convention, the first article of which related to the fisheries. By this article the United States "renounce forever, any liberty heretofore enjoyed or claimed by the inhabitants thereof to take, dry, or cure fish on or within three marine miles" of any of the "coasts, bays, creeks, or harbours" of the British dominions in America, not included within certain limits, within which the right to fish or to dry and cure fish was expressly reserved. It was provided, however, that the American fishermen might "enter such bays or harbours" for the purposes "of shelter and of repairing damages therein, of purchasing wood, and of obtaining water, and for no other purpose whatever," subject to such restrictions as might be necessary to prevent them from abusing the privileges thus reserved to them.

On June 14, 1819, an act, closely following the language of the article, was passed by the imperial parliament to carry it into effect; and from that time down to 1836, little trouble seems to have occurred. But in that year the legislature of Nova Scotia passed an act, by which the "hovering" of vessels within three miles of the coasts and harbors was sought to be prevented by various regulations and penalties; and claims were subsequently asserted to exclude American fishermen from all bays and even from all waters within lines drawn from headland to headland, to forbid them to navigate the Gut of Canso, and to deny them all privileges of traffic, including the purchase of bait and supplies in the British colonial ports. From 1839 down to 1854 there were numerous seizures, and in 1852 the home government sent over a force of war steamers and sailing vessels to assist in patrolling the coast.

With a view to adjust the various questions that had arisen, the British government in 1854 sent Lord Elgin to the United States on a special mission, and on June 5, 1854, he concluded with Mr. Marcy, who was then Secretary of State, a treaty in relation to the fisheries and to commerce and navigation. By this treaty the United States fishermen temporarily reacquired the greater part of the inshore privileges renounced by the convention of 1818. On the other hand, a reciprocal concession was granted to British fishermen on the eastern coasts of the United

States down to the thirty‑sixth parallel of north latitude, and provision was made for reciprocal free trade between the United States and the British colonies in North America in various articles of commerce. This treaty came into operation on March 16, 1855. It was terminated on March 17, 1866, on notice given by the United States in conformity with its provisions. All the old questions were thus revived; but a new arrangement was effected by Articles xviii.–xxv. of the comprehensive treaty of Washington of May 8, 1871. The American fishermen were again temporarily readmitted to the privileges renounced by the convention of 1818, while the United States agreed to admit Canadian fish and fish-oil free of duty, and to refer to a tribunal of arbitration, which was to meet at Halifax, the question of the amount of any additional compensation which should be paid by the United States for the inshore privileges. On November 23, 1877, an award was made in favor of Great Britain of the sum of five million five hundred thousand dollars, or nearly half a million dollars for each of the years during which the arrangement was necessarily to continue in force. The United States protested against the award, but paid it in due course. Lest, however, the same rate of compensation should subsequently be demanded, the United States in 1883 availed itself of the right to give notice of termination of the fishery articles, and they came to an end in 1885. A temporary arrangement was entered into for that year, under which the American fishermen continued to enjoy the privileges accorded them by the terminated articles, in consideration of President Cleveland's undertaking to recommend to Congress, when it should again assemble, the appointment of a joint commission to consider both the question of the fisheries and that of trade relations. The recommendation was submitted to Congress, but it was not adopted; and on the opening of the fishing season of 1886, seizures of American vessels began to be made. A sharp controversy followed, reviving questions not only as to the construction of the convention of 1818, but also as to the right of fishing vessels to participate in enlarged privileges of intercourse established since that time. What were the "bays" intended by the convention? Did they include only bodies of water not more than six marine miles wide at the mouth, or all bodies of water bearing the name of bays? Were the three marine miles to be measured from a line following the sinuosities of the coast, or from a line drawn from headland to headland, even where there might be no body of water bearing the name of a bay? Were American fishing vessels forbidden to traffic or to obtain supplies, even when they entered the colonial ports for one of the four purposes specified in the convention? All these questions were raised and elaborately argued. By an act of

March 3, 1887, Congress authorized the President in his discretion to adopt measures of retaliation. A negotiation was, however, subsequently undertaken, which resulted in the Bayard-Chamberlain treaty of February 15, 1888. Provision was made for delimiting the waters in which American fishermen were to be forbidden to fish. To this end, certain definite lines were expressly drawn; and, apart from these, the rule, followed in the North Sea and other fishery arrangements, was adopted, of treating as territorial waters all bays not more than ten miles wide at the mouth, the theory being that fishing could not be carried on in a free space of less than four miles, without constant danger of entering exclusive waters. Fishing vessels, when entering bays or harbors for any of the four purposes specified in the convention of 1818, were not to be required to enter or clear, unless remaining more than twenty-four hours or communicating with the shore, or to pay port dues or charges; and they were to be allowed to transship or sell their cargoes in case of distress or casualty, and to obtain on all occasions "casual or needful provisions and supplies," as distinguished from original outfits. Each vessel was to be duly numbered; but the penalty of forfeiture was to be imposed only for fishing in exclusive British waters, or for preparing in such waters to fish therein; and for any other violation of the fishery laws the penalty was not to exceed three dollars for every ton of the implicated vessel.

It was further stipulated that all restrictions should be removed from the purchase of bait, supplies, and outfits, the transshipment of catch, and the shipping of crews, whenever the United States should remove the duty from the fishery products of Canada and Newfoundland. This treaty enjoys the distinction of being the only one that was ever, by formal resolution of the Senate, discussed in open session, so that the speeches upon it may be found in the daily record of the Congressional debates. Late in August, 1888, after a long and animated debate, it was rejected. President Cleveland then recommended to Congress a definite course of retaliation, looking immediately to the suspension of the bonded-transit system. This recommendation failed; and a *modus vivendi*, which was arranged by the negotiators of the defeated treaty at the time of its signature, and under which a system of licenses was established, continued for the time being to operate by virtue of Canadian orders in council. The fisheries question was one of the subjects considered by the Quebec commission of 1898, but no conclusive results on any matter were reached by that body.

In its later phases, the discussion of the northeastern fisheries came to involve only to a comparatively slight extent any question as to the use of the open sea. Very different in that respect was the Bering Sea controversy, which arose in regard to the fur-seals in 1886. By an imperial ukase or edict of

July 8, 1799, Paul I. of Russia granted to the Russian-American Company various important rights on the Russian coasts in America, including that of fishing. Twenty-two years later—on September 7, 1821—there was issued by the Emperor Alexander another ukase, the apparent effect of which was much more far-reaching, since it purported to exclude foreigners from carrying on commerce and from whaling and fishing on the northwest coast of America, from Bering Strait down to the fifty-first parallel of north latitude, and forbade them even to approach within a hundred Italian miles of the coast. Against this ukase both the United States and Great Britain protested, and it was never enforced. On the other hand, a convention was concluded between the United States and Russia on April 17, 1824, by which it was agreed that "in any part of the great ocean, commonly called the Pacific Ocean, or South Sea," the citizens or subjects of the high contracting parties should be "neither disturbed nor restrained, either in navigation or in fishing." A treaty in similar terms was made by Great Britain in the following year. By a convention signed at Washington on March 30, 1867, the Russian Emperor, in consideration of the sum of seven million two hundred thousand dollars in gold, ceded "all the territory and dominion" which he possessed "on the continent of America and in the adjacent islands" to the United States. Of this cession, the eastern limit was that

defined in the treaty between Great Britain and
Russia of 1825. The western limit was defined by a
water line, which was drawn so as to include in the
territory conveyed numerous islands.

In 1886 certain Canadian sealers were seized by
United States revenue-cutters in Bering Sea, at a
distance of upwards of sixty miles from the nearest
land. The United States Court at Sitka pronounced
a sentence of condemnation, but the President subsequently ordered the vessels to be released; and on
August 17, 1887, Mr. Bayard, as Secretary of State,
instructed the American ministers at London, Paris,
and certain other capitals, to invite the governments
to which they were accredited to co-operate with the
United States in measures for the better protection
of the fur-seals. It was represented that, as the
result of indiscriminate killing, the seals were in
danger of extermination, and that the nations had a
common interest in preventing this from being done.
The responses to this overture were generally favorable, and negotiations with Great Britain had
practically reached a favorable conclusion, when, on
May 16, 1888, nine days after the adverse report of
the Committee on Foreign Relations of the United
States Senate on the Bayard-Chamberlain treaty,
they were arrested on an objection from the Canadian
government. On the 12th of the following September, Mr. E. J. Phelps, then American minister in London, in a despatch to Mr. Bayard, suggested that the

United States might of its own motion take measures to prevent the destruction of the fur-seals by capturing on the high seas the vessels employed in it. This suggestion was not then adopted; but, after the change of administration in 1889, seizures were renewed. A warm dispute followed, in which Mr. Blaine sought to defend the seizures on the ground that the killing of seals in the open sea was *contra bonos mores*, as well as on the supposition that Russia had asserted and exercised exclusive rights in Bering Sea, and that the treaties of 1824 and 1825 did not apply to that body of water. On February 29, 1892, however, a treaty was signed, by which a tribunal of arbitration,[1] to sit at Paris, was invested with power to decide: (1) what exclusive jurisdiction, or exclusive rights in the seal-fisheries, in Bering Sea, Russia asserted prior to the cession of Alaska to the United States; (2) how far those claims were recognized by Great Britain; (3) whether Bering Sea was included in the phrase "Pacific Ocean," as used in the treaties of 1824 and 1825; (4) whether all Russia's rights passed to the United States; and (5) whether the United States had any right of protection or property in the fur-seals in Bering Sea outside the ordinary three-mile limit. If the arbitrators found that the exclusive rights of the United States were insufficient, they were to determine what

---

[1] For the personnel of this tribunal see infra, p. 212.

concurrent regulations the two governments should jointly enforce outside territorial waters.

Before the tribunal of arbitration, the representatives of the United States relied much upon a theory of property in fur-seals; but on the various questions of right submitted, the decision of the arbitrators was adverse to the United States. This result was due, however, not to any lack of ability or of effort on the part of the accomplished American agent and counsel, who exhausted every resource of argument, but to certain historical and legal antecedents, among which we may mention the following:

1. That, when the first seizures were reported in 1886, the Department of State not only possessed no information concerning them, but was unable to give any explanation of them, and that, when the circumstances of the seizures were ascertained, even though the full judicial record had not then been received, the vessels were ordered to be released.

2. That the court in Alaska, in condemning the vessels and punishing their masters and crews, proceeded on a doctrine of *mare clausum*, which the United States had never legally asserted and which the government afterwards disavowed. It is indeed generally supposed, and the supposition apparently is shared by the Supreme Court, that Mr. Blaine in his correspondence claimed that the United States had derived from Russia exclusive dominion over Bering Sea. It is, however, a fact that in a note to Sir

Julian Pauncefote, December 17, 1890, Mr. Blaine said: "The government has never claimed it and never desired it; it expressly disavows it." Whether this sweeping denial is or is not altogether justified by the record, is a question that need not be here considered.

3. That the treaty ceding Alaska to the United States did not purport to convey the waters of Bering Sea, but in terms conveyed only "the territory and dominion" of Russia "on the continent of America and in the adjacent islands," and drew a water boundary so as to effect a transfer of the islands, many of them nameless, which lay in the intervening seas.

4. That the ukase of 1821, which contained the only distinctive claim of *mare clausum* ever put forward by Russia, did not assume to treat the whole of Bering Sea as a close sea, but only to exclude foreign vessels from coming within one hundred Italian miles of the coast, from the fifty-first parallel of north latitude to Bering Strait, without discrimination as to localities.

5. That against this ukase both the United States and Great Britain protested; and that by the treaties of 1824 and 1825 Russia agreed not to interfere with their citizens or subjects either in navigating or in fishing in "any part of the Pacific Ocean," thus abandoning the exclusive jurisdictional claim announced in the ukase.

6. That it was declared by Mr. Blaine in the diplomatic correspondence that if the phrase "Pacific Ocean," as used in those treaties, included Bering Sea, the United States had "no well-grounded complaint" against Great Britain; and that it was unanimously found by the arbitrators that the phrase Pacific Ocean did include Bering Sea.

7. That while the tribunal, by six voices to one, found that there was no evidence to substantiate the supposition that Russia had asserted exceptional claims as to the fur-seals, there was affirmative evidence that she had not done so in recent years. In reality, most of the specific passages from early Russian documents, given in the case of the United States to substantiate Russia's supposed exclusive claims, proved to be the interpolations of a dishonest translator, and were spontaneously withdrawn by the agent of the United States on his discovery of the circumstances, soon after the cases were exchanged. These interpolations, however, did not figure in the diplomatic correspondence, but were made after its close.

8. That it was admitted that no municipal law of the United States had ever treated the fur-seals, either individually or collectively, as the subject of property and protection on the high seas.

9. That it was also admitted by the representatives of the United States that, for the claim of property and protection on the high seas, there was

no precise precedent in international law, though it was strongly maintained that the claim was justified by analogies.

10. That the effort to support this claim was embarrassed by its relation to the subject of visitation and search on the high seas, and especially by the precedents which the United States itself had made on that subject.

The question of regulations stood on different grounds—that of international co-operation, proposed in 1887. The arbitrators, after deciding against the United States on questions of right, proceeded to prescribe regulations, which were afterwards duly put into operation by the two governments. Under a treaty of arbitration signed at Washington on February 8, 1896, the sum of $473,151.26 was awarded as compensation to be paid by the United States for interference with the Canadian-sealers.

V

THE CONTEST WITH COMMERCIAL RESTRICTIONS

WHEN viewed in their wider relations, the early efforts of the United States to establish the rights of neutrals and the freedom of the seas are seen to form a part of the great struggle for the liberation of commerce from the restrictions with which the spirit of national monopoly had fettered and confined it. When the United States declared their independence, exclusive restrictions, both in the exchange of commodities and in their transportation, existed on every side. The system of colonial monopoly was but the emanation of the general principle, on which nations then consistently acted, of regarding everything "bestowed on others as so much withholden from themselves." Prohibitions and discriminations were universal.

Such was the prospect on which the United States looked when they achieved their independence. With exceptions comparatively unimportant, there was not a single port in the Western Hemisphere with which an American vessel could lawfully trade, outside of its own country. But the exclusion most seriously felt was that from the British West Indies. Prior to the Revolution the burdens of the restrictive system were essentially mitigated by the intercolonial trade, the British colonists on the continent finding their best markets in the British islands; but when the United States, by establishing their independence, became to Great Britain a foreign nation, they at once collided with her colonial system. American statesmen foresaw these things and endeavored to guard against them, but in vain. When the provisional articles of peace with Great Britain were later converted into a definitive treaty, without the addition of any commercial clauses, the hope of establishing the relations between the two countries at the outset on the broad basis of mutual freedom of intercourse disappeared.

In the contest with commercial restrictions, the government of the United States adopted as the basis of its policy the principle of reciprocity. In its later diplomacy the term "reciprocity" is much used to denote agreements designed to increase the interchange of commodities by mutual or equivalent reductions of duty. Tested by recent experience, the later "reciprocity" might not inaptly be described as a policy recommended by free-traders as an escape from protection, and by protectionists as an escape from free trade, but distrusted by both and supported by neither. It is, however, impossible to doubt that, in the efforts of the United States to bring about the abolition of the cumbersome and obstructive contrivances of the old navigation laws, the policy of reciprocity proved to be an efficient instrument in furthering the tendency towards greater commercial freedom. It was announced by the government at the very threshold of its existence. In the preamble to the treaty of commerce with France of 1778, it was declared that the contracting parties, wishing to "fix in an equitable and permanent manner" the rules that should govern their commerce, had judged that this end "could not be better obtained than by taking for the basis of their agreement the most perfect equality and reciprocity, and by carefully avoiding all those burthensome preferences which are usually sources of debate, embarrassment, and discontent; by leaving, also, each party at liberty to make, respecting commerce and navigation, those interior regulations which it shall find most convenient to itself; and by founding the advantage of commerce solely upon reciprocal utility and the just rules of free intercourse; reserving withal to each party the liberty of admitting at its pleasure other nations to a participation of the same advantages." John Quincy Adams, in 1823, while avowing the belief that this preamble was "the first instance on the diplomatic record of nations, upon which the true principles of all fair commercial negotiation between independent states were laid down and proclaimed to the world," at the same time declared that it "was, to the foundation of our commercial intercourse with the rest of mankind, what the Declaration of Independence was to that of our internal government. The two instruments," he added, "were parts of one and the same system matured by long and anxious deliberation of the founders of this Union in the ever memorable Congress of 1776; and as the Declaration of Independence was the foundation of all our municipal institutions, the preamble to the treaty with France laid the corner-stone for all our subsequent transactions of intercourse with foreign nations."

The progress of the United States, in the contest thus early begun with commercial restrictions, was painful and slow. Soon after the establishment of independence, Congress took into consideration the entire subject of commercial relations, and on May 7, 1784, adopted a series of resolutions in which the principles by which American negotiators should be guided were set forth. By the first of these resolutions it was declared that, in any arrangements that might be effected, each party should have the right to carry its own produce, manufactures, and merchandise in its own vessels to the ports of the other, and to bring thence the produce and merchandise of the other, paying in each case only such duties as were paid by the most-favored nation. The second resolution, which related to colonial trade, embodied the proposal that a direct and similar intercourse should be permitted between the United States and the possessions of European powers in America, or at any rate between the United States and certain free ports in such possessions; and that, if neither of these alternatives could be obtained, then each side should at least be permitted to carry its own produce and merchandise in its own vessels directly to the other. When the wars growing out of the French Revolution began, no progress had been made by the United States towards the attainment of the objects of the second resolution. American vessels laden with the produce of their own country, and in some cases when laden with the produce of other countries, were admitted into most of the European ports, including those of Great Britain, on condition of paying the customary alien dues; but the ports of the colonies continued to be closed against them, while some of the most important American products were specifically excluded from the trade which vessels of the dominant country were permitted to carry on between its colonies and the United States. When authorizing Gouverneur Morris, as an informal agent, in 1789, to sound the views of the British ministry concerning relations with the United States, Washington said: "Let it be strongly impressed on your mind that the privilege of carrying our productions in our vessels to their islands, and bringing in return the productions of those islands to our own ports and markets, is regarded here as of the highest importance; and you will be careful not to countenance any idea of our dispensing with it in a treaty." In the following year Morris reported that no arrangement on the subject could be made. The question was, however, revived in the instructions given to Jay, as special plenipotentiary to England, on May 6, 1794. He was directed to secure for American vessels the privilege of carrying between the United States and the British West Indies the same articles as might be transported between the two places in British bottoms, and, unless he could obtain this, he was to do no more than refer to his government such concessions as might be offered. He submitted to Lord Grenville a proposal in this sense, but, although it was limited to American vessels of not more than a hundred tons burden, it was rejected. So important, however, did Jay conceive it to be to obtain some relief from the colonial restrictions that, in spite of his instructions, he assented to the incorporation into the treaty, which was signed by him and Lord Grenville on November 19, 1794, of an article by which the privilege of trading between the United States and the British West Indies was for a term of years extended to American vessels of a burden of not more than seventy tons, but only on condition that, during the continuance of the privilege, the United States should prohibit and restrain the carrying of any molasses, sugar, coffee, cocoa, or cotton in American vessels, either from the British islands or from the United States itself, to any port not in the United States. It was argued that this condition, by which American vessels were to be forbidden to transport from their own country any of the specified commodities, even though produced there or in a third country, was essential as a safeguard against abuse of the treaty privilege. American vessels, it was said, might, after importing a cargo from the British islands, carry it on to Europe, under the guise of a feigned American product, and thus destroy the exclusive advantages which were to continue to belong to British shipping. But the price was deemed by the United States to be too high for the limited privilege that was gained. The Senate, in assenting to the ratification of the treaty, struck out the obnoxious article. The treaty, however, provided that the citizens of the two countries might freely pass and repass by land, or by inland navigation, into the territories of the one and the other on the continent of America (the country within the limits of the Hudson's Bay Company only excepted), and carry on trade and commerce with each other in that way. American vessels were expressly excluded from any seaports in such territories; but, by another article of the treaty, they were admitted on certain conditions to a direct trade with the British dominions in the East Indies.

During the long wars that grew out of the French Revolution, colonial restrictions in America were from time to time suspended under military necessity. The home governments, when unable to carry on the trade under their own flag, were at times reluctantly obliged to open it to neutral ships in order that it might not perish altogether. As early as March 26, 1793, the ports of the French colonies in America were opened on certain terms to the vessels of neutral countries. On June 9, 1793, Spain opened the ports of New Orleans, Pensacola, and St. Augustine to friendly commerce, but foreign vessels were required to touch at Corcubion, in Galicia, or at Alicant, and obtain a permit, without which no entry into the specified ports was allowed. Seventeen years later there began, in a conservative revolt against the Napoleonic domination in Spain, the movement in the Spanish colonies in America that was gradually to be transformed into a genuine struggle for independence, a struggle that was to end in the liberation of Spain's vast continental domain in the Western Hemisphere from the bonds of colonial monopoly. With the concurrent independence of Portugal's great colony, Brazil, the system for the most part disappeared from the American continents, below the northern boundary of the United States. But, emerging from the long Napoleonic struggle triumphant, Great Britain retained her authority over her colonies, and had even added to their number. With her the question of colonial restrictions therefore still remained. It had never ceased, except during the war of 1812, to be a subject of consideration. Monroe and Pinkney had vainly endeavored to settle it in 1806. After the ratification of the treaty of Ghent, the discussion was resumed. John Quincy Adams, with his accustomed energy and dialectic force; Richard Rush, with his wonted tact and wise judgment, and Albert Gallatin, with all his penetrating and persuasive reasonableness, had all essayed to arrange it, but without avail. In 1817, Lord Castlereagh proposed to extend to the United States the provisions of the "free port" acts, the effect of which would have been to admit to a limited trade American vessels of one deck; but this proposal was rejected, and by the act of Congress of April 18, 1818, the ports of the United States were closed against British vessels coming from any British colony which was, by the ordinary laws of navigation and trade, closed against American vessels; and British vessels sailing from the United States were put under bond to land their cargoes elsewhere than in such a colony. By an act of May 15, 1820, these restrictions were specifically made applicable to any British colonial port in the West Indies or America. In 1822 these restrictions were partially suspended, in reciprocal recognition of the opening of certain colonial ports to American vessels under certain conditions. By the act of Congress of March 1, 1823, this suspension was continued, but a claim was also put forth, which had previously been advanced by the United States in negotiation but had always been resisted by Great Britain, that no higher duties should be imposed in the colonial ports on articles imported from the United States in American vessels, than on similar articles when imported in British ships from any country whatsoever, including Great Britain herself and her colonies. This claim had been a favorite one with Mr. Adams, on the supposition that its acceptance was necessary to assure to American vessels their full share of the carrying-trade; and it was now proposed to enforce it by means of discriminating duties. Its attempted enforcement immediately led to the imposition of countervailing duties by Great Britain. Such was the condition of things when, by the act of July 5, 1825, Parliament opened the trade with the British colonies in North America and the West Indies to the vessels of all nations, on specified conditions. The government of the United States failed to accept these conditions, with the result that on December 1, 1826, direct intercourse between the United States and the British-American colonies, in British as well as in American vessels, was almost wholly suspended.

In learning how an escape was found from this dilemma, we shall see how the unmaking of a minister contributed to the making of a President. When Andrew Jackson was inaugurated as President, in 1829, Martin Van Buren became his Secretary of State, and Louis McLane was sent as minister to the court of St. James. In a speech in the Senate in February, 1827, Van Buren had criticised the administration then in power for its omission to accept the conditions prescribed in the act of Parliament of 1825. The views which he then expressed he embodied on July 20, 1829, in an instruction to McLane. In concluding a long and able review of the controversy with Great Britain, Van Buren declared that there were three grounds on which the United States was assailable. The first was "in our too long and too tenaciously resisting the right of Great Britain to impose protecting duties in her colonies"; the second, "in not relieving her vessels from the restriction of returning direct from the United States to the colonies, after permission had been given by Great Britain to our vessels to clear out from the colonies to any other than a British port"; and the third, "in omitting to accept the terms offered by the act of Parliament of July, 1825." McLane was authorized to say that the United States would open its ports to British vessels coming from the British colonies laden with such colonial products as might be im-

ported in American vessels, on condition that Great
Britain would extend to American vessels the privi
leges offered by that act. In these instructions Van
Buren only re-echoed the views which Gallatin had
strongly expressed to the Department of State in his
despatches in 1826. But Van Buren did not stop
here. He directed McLane not to "harass" the
British cabinet by the repetition of prior discussions,
but, if the course of the late administration should
be brought up, to say that its views had been sub
mitted to the people of the United States, that the
counsels by which his own conduct was directed
represented the judgment expressed by the only
earthly tribunal to which the late administration
was amenable for its acts, and that to set up those
acts as the cause of withholding from the people
of the United States privileges, which would other
wise be extended to them, would be unjust in itself
and could not fail to excite their deepest sensibility
McLane duly communicated to the British govern
ment the entire purport of his instructions. His
negotiations were altogether successful. By a proc
lamation issued by President Jackson on October
5, 1830, under the authority of an act of Congress
of the 29th of the preceding May, the ports of the
United States were declared to be open to British
vessels and their cargoes coming from the colonies
on payment of the same charges as American ves
sels coming from the same quarter. An order in

council issued November 5, 1830, extended to American vessels reciprocal privileges. The last remnants of the vicious system that was thus broken down were removed in 1849.

In 1831 McLane resigned his post in London, and Van Buren was appointed by the President to fill the vacancy. He arrived in England in September, and entered upon the discharge of the duties of his office. On January 25, 1832, the Senate, of which he had so recently been a member, refused to confirm him. In the memorable debate that preceded his rejection, his pointed and censorious disavowal, in the instructions to McLane, of responsibility for the acts of the preceding administration, formed a principal ground of objection. It was eloquently declared by his Whig opponents that party differences should not be injected into international discussions. The criticism was essentially sound; but, in the popular estimation, the punishment was altogether disproportionate to the offence. A widespread impression that its infliction was inspired by resentment, occasioned by party defeat, greatly enhanced Van Buren's political strength.

While the contest with colonial restrictions was going on, steady progress was made towards the accomplishment of the design, propounded by the Continental Congress in 1776, of placing the foreigner, in respect of commerce and navigation, on an equal footing with the native, and to this end of abolishing all discriminating charges whatsoever. "This principle," once declared John Quincy Adams, "is altogether congenial to our institutions, and the main obstacle to its adoption consists in this: that the fairness of its operation depends upon its being admitted universally." Before the formation of the Constitution, the several States were driven for purposes of retaliation to impose discriminating duties on foreign vessels and their cargoes. The system was continued by the government of the United States, for the same reason. By an act of March 3, 1815, however, Congress offered to abolish all discriminating duties, both of tonnage and of impost, on foreign vessels laden with the produce or manufactures of their own country, on condition of the concession of a reciprocal privilege to American vessels. By "discriminating duties" are meant all duties in excess of what would be charged, in the particular country, one of its own vessels and the cargo imported in it. This principle first found conventional expression in the treaty of commerce and navigation with Great Britain of July 3, 1815; but its operation was therein confined, on the part of that power, to the British territories in Europe. By the act of Congress of March 1, 1817, the offer made in the act of 1815 was enlarged, by including vessels belonging to citizens either of the country by which the goods were produced or manufactured, or of the country from which they could only be, or most usually were, first shipped for transportation. The final step was taken in the act of March 24, 1828, which is still in force, and by which a standing offer was made for the reciprocal abolition of all discriminating duties, without regard to the origin of the cargo or the port from which the vessel came. The provisions of this statute have been extended to many countries by proclamation, and the principle on which they are founded is confirmed by numerous treaties.

With the passing away of the old system of exclusions and discriminations in the West, the activities of American diplomacy were directed more and more to the East, where the expansion of commerce was hindered by various conditions, presenting every phase of obstruction from general insecurity to positive non-intercourse. In 1830 a treaty of commerce and navigation was concluded with the Ottoman Empire, with which a trade had been carried on under the somewhat costly shelter of the English Levant Company. But a wider field awaited the spirit of enterprise in the Far East. In August, 1784, less than a year after the definitive peace with Great Britain, a New York ship, the *Empress of China*, bore the American flag into Canton. Before the close of the century, American vessels had prosecuted their adventures in trading and in fishing into all parts of the Pacific. It was an American ship, fitted out at Boston for the fur-trade, that entered and explored in 1792 the "River of the West" and gave to it its name, Columbia. Even the stern barriers of Spanish colonial exclusion failed to withstand the assaults of American energy in the trade carried on between the shores of America and the shores of Asia. In time, private initiative was powerfully reinforced by the action of government. In 1832 Edmund Roberts, a sea-captain of Portsmouth, New Hampshire, was appointed by President Jackson as "agent for the purpose of examining in the Indian Ocean the means of extending the commerce of the United States by commercial arrangements with the powers whose dominions border on those seas." Taking with him blank letters of credence, he embarked in March, 1832, on the sloop-of-war, *Peacock*, for his long voyage of inquiry and negotiation. If we were to judge by the provision made for his comfort and remuneration, we should infer that little importance was attached to his mission. Rated on the *Peacock* as "captain's clerk," his pay was barely sufficient to defray the cost of an insurance on his life for the benefit of his numerous children; and for three months he was obliged to lie on the sea-washed gun-deck with the crew, all the available space in the cabin being occupied by a *chargé d'affaires* to Buenos Ayres whose name is now forgotten. He touched at all the important countries eastward of the Cape of Good Hope, except those on the Bay of Bengal. He visited Java three times, on one occasion remaining at Batavia nearly two months. At Manila, where the crew were attacked by cholera, the *Peacock* was compelled to put to sea with her deck converted into a hospital. In Siam, and in the countries bordering on the Persian Gulf and the Red Sea, Roberts endured many hardships and encountered many perils. But his sacrifices were not in vain. On March 30, 1833, he concluded a treaty of amity and commerce with Siam, and on September 21st signed a similar treaty with the Sultan of Muscat. He returned to the United States, in 1834, on the U. S. S. *Lexington*. His treaties were promptly approved by the Senate. He then returned to the East, sailing again in a man-of-war. His diplomatic career ended in 1836, at Macao, where he fell a victim to the plague. In 1839 Congress, recognizing the gross inadequacy of the recompense that had been made for his exceptional services, granted to his legal representatives a belated requital. If the successful performance of important public duties, unhampered by any thought of personal aggrandizement, forms a just title to remembrance, there can be no doubt that an abiding place in our history belongs to this pioneer of American diplomacy in Asia.

Roberts was empowered to negotiate a treaty with Cochin China, but in this task he made no progress. In all the vast Chinese Empire only one port

—that of Canton—was accessible to foreign merchants. The first permanent breach in the wall of seclusion was made by the treaty between Great Britain and China, signed at Nanking, August 29, 1842, at the close of the opium war. By this treaty the ports of Canton, Amoy, Foochow, Ningpo, and Shanghai were opened to British subjects and their commerce, and the island of Hongkong was ceded to Great Britain as an entrepôt. A supplementary treaty of commerce and navigation was concluded in the following year. The United States soon appeared in the breach. By the act of Congress of March 3, 1843, the sum of forty thousand dollars was placed at the disposal of the President to enable him to establish commercial relations with China on terms of "national equal reciprocity." On May 8th, Caleb Cushing, of Massachusetts, was appointed to the mission with the title of minister plenipotentiary and commissioner. The choice was fortunate. No public character in America has possessed a mind more versatile or talents more varied than Cushing. Lawyer, jurist, politician, soldier, and diplomatist, a student of literature and of science, and an accomplished linguist, he responded to the demands of every situation, promptly and without embarrassment. So prodigious and insatiable was his acquisitiveness that, as the tradition runs in the Department of State, when deprived of other mental pabulum he would memorize the

CALEB CUSHING.

groups of figures in the cipher code. When he set out for China, a squadron of three vessels was placed at his disposal. On February 27, 1844, writing from the flag-ship *Brandywine*, in Macao Roads, he announced to the governor-general of the two Kwang provinces his arrival with full powers to make a treaty. He encountered the usual evasions; but, after an exchange of correspondence, he learned early in May that Tsiyeng, the negotiator of the treaties with Great Britain, had been appointed as imperial commissioner to treat with him. Tsiyeng arrived outside Macao on June 16th, and next day entered the village of Wang Hiya, where with his suite he lodged in a temple that had been prepared for him. On June 21st, after an exchange of official visits, Cushing submitted a project of a treaty. In communicating it he stated that his government desired to treat on the basis of "cordial friendship and firm peace," that it did not desire any part of the territory of China, and that, while it would be happy to treat on the basis of opening all ports, yet, if China so desired, it would be content with a free and secure commerce with the five ports opened by the British treaty. The negotiations proceeded steadily, and on July 3, 1844, a treaty was signed. The point of diplomatic representation at Peking was yielded with the express understanding that, in case it should be conceded to other Western powers, the envoy of the United States should likewise be received. All the commercial privileges obtained by Great Britain for her subjects were, with some variations, extended to citizens of the United States; and American citizens were, like British subjects, exempted from Chinese jurisdiction. A curious light is thrown on American enterprise by a correspondence which Cushing, before his return to the United States, had with two American citizens who had established a ship-yard on the Chinese coast, opposite Hongkong, and who had been ordered away. Cushing advised them to acquiesce in the action of the Chinese authorities, in view of the stipulations of the treaty which he had just concluded.

A new treaty was made in 1858; and ten years later a special Chinese embassy, headed by Anson Burlingame, signed at Washington the treaty that is known by his name. In entering the service of China, after a notable career of six years as American minister at Peking, Burlingame declared that he was governed by the interests of his country and of civilization; and his course was approved by his government. The rule that the United States will not receive as a diplomatic representative of a foreign power one of its own citizens was in his case gladly waived. As American minister at Peking, he sought "to substitute fair diplomatic action in China for force," a policy which Mr. Seward "approved with much commendation." Through the vicissitudes of the years that have since elapsed it may be said that the United States has, in its commercial dealings with China, uniformly adhered to that principle. In his celebrated circular of July 3, 1900, during the military advance of the powers for the relief of their beleagured legations in Peking, Mr. Hay declared it to be the policy of the United States "to seek a solution which may bring about permanent safety and peace to China, preserve China's territorial and administrative entity, protect all rights guaranteed to friendly powers by treaties and international law, and safeguard for the world the principle of equal and impartial trade with all parts of the Chinese Empire." This declaration admirably sums up what have been conceived to be the cardinal principles of American policy in the Far East. In the acquisition of the Philippines, the United States declared its purpose to maintain in those islands "an open door to the world's commerce." The phrase "open door" is but a condensed expression of "the principle of equal and impartial trade" for all nations. Its meaning was well illustrated by the stipulation in the treaty of peace with Spain that the United States would, for the term of ten years, "admit Spanish ships and merchandise to the ports of the Philippine Islands on the same terms as ships and merchandise of the United States."

When Edmund Roberts was despatched to the

East, he was directed to obtain information respecting Japan and the value of its trade with the Dutch and the Chinese. Japan, like China, had been closed to intercourse with the Western powers in the seventeenth century, chiefly on account of foreign aggressions. The seclusion of Japan was, however, even more complete than that of China, since the only privilege of trade conceded to any Western power was that granted to the Dutch, who maintained a factory on the island of Deshima, at Nagasaki, and who were allowed to fit out two ships a year from Batavia to that port. In 1845 Alexander Everett, when he went as commissioner to China, took with him a full power to negotiate a treaty with Japan. This power he afterwards transferred to Commodore James Biddle, who in 1846 paid an ill-fated visit to the bay of Yedo. In 1849 Commander Glynn, of the United States navy, while stationed in the western Pacific, made a voyage in the *Preble* to Nagasaki to inquire as to the fate of certain American whalers, said to have been shipwrecked, who were reported to be held as prisoners by the Japanese. Commander Glynn found that the men were in reality deserters, but he obtained their release; and on his return to the United States he urged that another effort be made to open an intercourse between the two countries, especially with a view to the use of a Japanese port for the accommodation of a line of steamers which was then expected to be established between California and China. On June 10, 1851, Commodore Aulick was instructed to proceed to Yedo in his flag-ship, accompanied by as many vessels of his squadron as might be conveniently employed. His health, however, soon afterwards became impaired, and he was relieved of the mission. His powers were then transferred to Commodore Matthew C. Perry, by whom elaborate preparations were made for the expedition.

On the afternoon of Friday, July 8, 1853, Perry, in command of a squadron of four vessels, anchored in the bay of Yedo. His proceedings were characterized by energy and decision. He had, as he said, determined to demand as a right and not to solicit as a favor those acts of courtesy which are due from one civilized nation to another, and to allow none of the petty annoyances that had been unspairingly visited on those who had preceded him. He declined to deliver his credentials to any but an officer of the highest rank. When he was asked to go to Nagasaki, he refused; when ordered to leave the bay, he moved higher up; and he found that the nearer he approached the imperial city "the more polite and friendly they became." After delivering his letters to two princes designated by the Emperor to receive them, he went away, announcing that he would return in the following spring to receive a reply to his propositions. He returned with redoubled forces in February, 1854, and, passing by the city of Uraga, anchored not far below Yedo. The Emperor had appointed commissioners to treat with him, four of whom were princes of the empire. They desired him to return to Uraga, but he declined to do so. The commissioners then consented to treat at a place opposite the ships. Here the Japanese erected a pavilion, and on March 8th Perry landed in state, with an escort of five hundred officers, seamen, and marines, embarked in twenty-seven barges. "With people of forms," said Perry, "it is necessary either to set all ceremony aside, or to out-Herod Herod in assumed personal consequence and ostentation. I have adopted the two extremes." Perry submitted a draught of a treaty; and, pending the negotiations, he established a telegraph-line on shore, and laid down and put in operation a railway with a locomotive and cars, "carrying around the circle many of the astonished natives." A treaty was signed on March 31, 1854. American ships were allowed to obtain provisions and coal and other necessary supplies at Simoda and Hakodate, and aid and protection in case of shipwreck were promised. No provision for commercial intercourse was secured, but the privilege was obtained of appointing a consul to reside at Simoda. Such was the first opening of Japan, after two centuries of seclusion. On July 17, 1901, there was unveiled at Kurihama, a monument in com-

MATTHEW C. PERRY, U. S. N.

memoration of Perry's advent. In Japan his name is to-day a household word, and is better known than that of any other foreigner.

On September 8, 1855, the government of the United States, availing itself of the privilege secured by the Perry treaty, appointed Townsend Harris as consul-general to reside at Simoda. He was chosen in the hope that by reason of his knowledge of Eastern character and his general intelligence and experience in business, he might be able to induce the Japanese to enter into a treaty of commerce. On July 29, 1858, his efforts were crowned with success. A provision for diplomatic representation at Yedo was obtained; rights of residence and of trade at certain ports were secured; duties were regulated; the privilege of extraterritoriality was granted to Americans in Japan; and religious freedom in that country was promised. Harris's triumph was won by a firm, tactful, honest diplomacy, and without the aid of a fleet, though it was no doubt true that he invoked the then recent humiliation of China by the European allies as an argument in favor of a voluntary intercourse. Before the end of the year, the fleets of the allies appeared in Japanese waters, and treaties similar to that of the United States were obtained by France and Great Britain. Treaties between Japan and other powers followed in due time. Harris's treaty provided for the exchange of ratifications at Washington. For this purpose the Japanese government sent a special embassy to the United States. Including servants, it comprised seventy-one persons. They were conveyed to America in a United States man-of-war, and Congress provided for their expenses. The ratifications of the treaty were exchanged at Washington on May 22, 1860, and the members of the embassy were afterwards conducted to some of the principal American cities. They were sent back to Japan on the man-of-war *Niagara*. To the shallow and sectarian reasoner, the Japan of to-day, once more possessed of full judicial and economic autonomy, and in the potent exercise of all the rights of sovereignty, presents an astounding spectacle of sudden, if not miraculous development; but in reality Japan is an ancient and polished nation, the roots of whose civilization, though its outward forms may have changed, strike deep into the past.

Corea, the Land of the Morning Calm, continued, long after the opening of China and Japan, to observe a rigorous seclusion. Efforts to secure access had invariably ended in disaster. On May 20, 1882, however, Commodore Shufeldt, U. S. N., invested with diplomatic powers, succeeded, with the friendly good offices of Li Hung-Chang, in concluding with the Hermit Kingdom the first treaty made by it with a Western power. The last great barrier of national non-intercourse was broken down, and, no matter what may be Corea's ultimate fate, is not likely to be restored.

VI

NON-INTERVENTION AND THE MONROE DOCTRINE

AMONG the rules of conduct prescribed for the United States by the statesmen who formulated its foreign policy, none was conceived to be more fundamental or more distinctively American than that which forbade intervention in the political affairs of other nations. The right of the government to intervene for the protection of its citizens in foreign lands and on the high seas never was doubted; nor was such action withheld in proper cases. But, warned by the spectacle of the great European struggles that had marked the attempts of nations to control one another's political destiny, the statesmen of America, believing that they had a different mission to perform, planted themselves upon the principle of the equality of nations as expounded by Grotius and other masters of international law. This principle was expressed with peculiar felicity and force by Vattel, who declared that nations inherited from nature "the same obligations and rights," that power or weakness could not in this respect produce any difference, and that a "small republic" was "no less a sovereign state than the most powerful kingdom." The same thought was tersely phrased by Chief-Justice Marshall, in his celebrated affirmation: "No principle is more universally acknowledged than the perfect equality of nations. Russia and Geneva have equal rights." And as the Declaration of Independence proclaimed life, liberty, and the pursuit of happiness to be "inalienable rights" of individual men, so the founders of the American republic ascribed the same rights to men in their aggregate political capacity as independent nations.

While the principle of non-intervention formed an integral part of the political philosophy of American statesmen, its practical importance was profoundly impressed upon them by the narrowness of their escape from being drawn, by the alliance with France, into the vortex of the European conflicts that grew out of the French Revolution. Even before American independence was acknowledged by Great Britain, American statesmen scented the dangers that lurked in a possible implication in European broils. "You are afraid," said Richard Oswald to John Adams, "of being made the tool of the powers of Europe." "Indeed, I am," said Adams. "What powers?" inquired Oswald. "All of them," replied Adams; "it is obvious that all the powers of Europe will be continually manoeuvring with us to work us into their real or imaginary balances of power. . . . But I think that it ought to be our rule not to meddle." In 1793, the revolutionary government of France, apparently doubting the applicability of the existing alliance with the United States to the situation in Europe, submitted a proposal for "a national agreement, in which two great peoples shall suspend their commercial and political interests and establish a mutual understanding to defend the empire of liberty, wherever it can be embraced." This proposal the American government declined; and its response found practical embodiment in its acts. The reasons for the policy of non-intervention and neutrality, to which the administration of the time so sedulously adhered, were eloquently summed up by Washington in that immortal political legacy, his Farewell Address. "The great rule of conduct for us, in regard to foreign nations," said Washington, "is, in extending our commercial relations, to have with them as little political connection as possible. So far as we have already formed engagements, let them be fulfilled with perfect good faith. Here let us stop." The same thought was conveyed by Jefferson, in his first inaugural address, in the apothegm— "Peace, commerce, and honest friendship with all nations, entangling alliances with none."

The policy of non-intervention embraced matters of religion as well as of politics. By the first amendment to the Constitution of the United States, Congress was expressly forbidden to make any law "respecting an establishment of religion, or prohibiting the free exercise thereof." This inhibition against governmental interference with religious opinions and practices was in its spirit extended to the intercourse of the United States with foreign nations. In Article ix. of the treaty between the United States and Tripoli, which was concluded on November 4, 1796, during the administration of Washington, we find this significant declaration: "As the Government of the United States of America is not in any sense founded on the Christian Religion; as it has in itself no character of enmity against the laws, religion, or tranquillity of Mussulmen, . . . it is declared by the parties, that no pretext arising from religious opinions shall ever produce an interruption of the harmony existing between the two countries." With the omission of the introductory phrase, a similar declaration was inserted in the treaty with Tripoli of 1805, and in the treaties with Algiers of 1815 and 1816. A stipulation less broad in its tolerance appears in Article xxix. of the treaty between the United States and China, signed at Tientsin, June 18, 1858. This article, after reciting that the principles of the Christian religion are "recognized as teaching men to do good, and to do to others as they would have others do to them," provides that "any person, whether citizen of the United States or Chinese convert, who, ac-

134

JAMES MONROE

cording to these tenets, peaceably teach and practice the principles of Christianity, shall in no case be interfered with or molested." By Article iv., however, of the Burlingame treaty of 1868, this stipulation is mentioned as an introduction to the declaration that it is "further agreed that citizens of the United States in China of every religious persuasion, and Chinese subjects in the United States, shall enjoy entire liberty of conscience, and shall be exempt from all disability or persecution on account of their religious faith or worship in either country." In harmony with this principle was the simple declaration in the treaty with Siam of 1856, and in the treaty with Japan of 1858, that Americans in those countries should "be allowed the free exercise of their religion." They were to be protected, not as the adherents or the propagandists of any particular faith, but as American citizens. As was well said by Mr. Cass, it was the object of the United States "not merely to protect a Catholic in a Protestant country, a Protestant in a Catholic country, a Jew in a Christian country, but an American in all countries."

The policy of non-intervention, which guided the United States during the wars growing out of the French Revolution, was severely tested in the struggle of the Spanish colonies in America for independence; but, under the guardian care of Monroe and John Quincy Adams, it was scrupulously adhered to. In view of this circumstance, it is strange that one of the gravest perils by which, after the days of the alliance with France, the maintenance of the policy was ever apparently threatened should have grown out of a political contest in Europe. The struggle of the Greeks for independence evoked much sympathy in America as well as in England; but the struggle of the Hungarians, under the leadership of Kossuth, for emancipation from Austrian rule, gave rise in the United States to manifestations of feeling that were unprecedented. The Hungarian revolution came at a time when the spirit of democracy, which distinguishes the political and social development of the nineteenth century, was especially active; but the wide-spread interest felt in the United States in the Hungarian movement was greatly intensified by reason of the popular assumption that the declaration of Hungary's independence, although it in reality left the question of a permanent form of government wholly in abeyance, was the forerunner of a republic. It was, however, only after the arrival of Kossuth in the United States that the excitement reached its greatest height. In June, 1849, Mr. A. Dudley Mann was appointed by the President as a "special and confidential agent of the United States to Hungary"; but, before he reached his destination, Russia had intervened in aid of Austria, and the revolution had practically come to an end. When the revolution

was crushed, Kossuth and many of his associates
sought refuge in Turkey. By a joint resolution of
Congress of March 3, 1851, the President was requested, if it should be the wish of these exiles to
"emigrate" to the United States, to authorize the
employment of a public vessel to convey them to
America. In conformity with this request the
U. S. S. *Mississippi* was sent to the Dardanelles; but
the exiles had scarcely embarked, when it was found
that Kossuth had other views than that of coming
to America as an emigrant. At Gibraltar he left
the *Mississippi* and proceeded to London, for the
purpose of conferring with revolutionary exiles in
that city; and he afterwards sailed for America in
the steamer *Humboldt*, from Southampton. He arrived at New York on the night of December 14,
1851, after a stormy passage. He soon dissipated
all doubts as to the objects of his mission. In his
public addresses he cast off all reserve, and in his
"official capacity" as the representative of Hungary made an appeal for aid. He affirmed that the
consideration of distance should not deter the United
States in the case of Hungary any more than in that
of Cuba from interfering against European invasion.
Cuba was six days' distant from New York; Hungary was eighteen. Was this, he asked, a circumstance to regulate the conduct and policy of a great
people? The people, wherever he went, seemed
enthusiastically to give a negative answer. His

journey to Washington was in the nature of a triumphal progress. When presented to the President, he made a direct appeal for intervention. President Fillmore, with courtesy and dignity, but with equal candor, repelled the solicitation. But, for his disappointment at the White House, Kossuth found consolation in his reception by Congress, though it in the end proved to be wholly illusory. He was received both by the Senate and by the House, and was banqueted by Congress. The first effective check to the popular excitement was given by Henry Clay, who refused to countenance the prevailing agitation. Kossuth more than once expressed a desire to meet him, and Clay, though in feeble health, at length granted him an interview. "For the sake of my country," said Clay, addressing Kossuth, "you must allow me to protest against the policy you propose to her." "Waiving the grave and momentous question of the right of one nation to assume the executive power among nations, for the enforcement of international law," Clay pointed out the practical difficulties that stood in the way of affording to Hungary effective aid against Austria and Russia. He also enlarged upon the evil example that would be afforded by the United States to other powers in departing from its "ancient policy of amity and non-intervention"; and, after declaring that the United States had, by adhering to that policy, "done more for the cause of liberty in the world than arms could effect," he concluded: "Far better is it for ourselves, for Hungary, and for the cause of liberty, that, adhering to our wise pacific system and avoiding the distant wars of Europe, we should keep our lamp burning brightly on this Western shore, as a light to all nations, than to hazard its utter extinction, amid the ruins of fallen or falling republics in Europe." The Kossuth danger passed away even more suddenly than it had arisen. After he left Washington, he addressed a letter to the presiding officers of the two houses of Congress, in which he expressed the hope that the United States would pronounce in favor of the law of nations and of international rights and duties. A motion to print this letter was carried in the Senate by only one vote, and the arguments in support of the motion were almost exclusively confined to considerations of courtesy. Indeed, the sudden collapse of Kossuth enthusiasm in high places, after his departure from the capital, would have been inexplicable if the open opponents of his policy of intervention had found any one to meet them on that ground.

It may be said that the most pronounced exception ever made by the United States, apart from cases arising under the Monroe Doctrine, to its policy of non-intervention, is that which was made in the case of Cuba. At various times, since the United States became an independent nation, con-

ditions in Cuba had been such as to invite interference either for the purpose of correcting dis-
orders which existed there, or for the purpose of
preventing Cuba from falling a prey to some of
Spain's European enemies. During the Ten Years'
War in Cuba, from 1868 till 1878, intervention by
the United States was prevented on several occasions only by the powerful influence of President
Grant, counselled and supported by his Secretary
of State, Hamilton Fish. In its abstention, the
administration was aided by the situation at home,
which afforded daily admonition of the difficulties
that might attend the re-establishment of order
in a large and populous island where the process
of emancipation was still going on. In 1895 the
situation was changed in the United States as
well as in Cuba. American interests in the island
had also increased. The second insurrection was,
besides, more active than the first, and spread over
a wider area. If the conflict were left to take its
course, the ruin of the island was apparently assured. The United States tendered its good offices;
but the offer was not productive of any tangible result. In his annual message of December 7, 1896,
President Cleveland declared that, when Spain's
inability to suppress the insurrection had become
manifest, and the struggle had degenerated into a
hopeless strife involving useless sacrifice of life and
the destruction of the very subject-matter of the

HAMILTON FISH

conflict, a situation would be presented in which the obligation to recognize the sovereignty of Spain would be "superseded by higher obligations." Conditions continued to grow worse. The distress produced by the measures of concentration, under the rule of General Weyler, excited strong feeling in the United States, and prompted President McKinley to request Spain to put an end to existing conditions and restore order. General Weyler was afterwards succeeded by General Blanco, and it was announced that an autonomous régime would be instituted. But neither the offer of autonomy nor the actual institution of an autonomous government produced peace. The insurgents, embittered by the three years' conflict, rejected the programme of autonomy with substantial unanimity, while the distinctively Spanish element of the population viewed it with disapprobation and withdrew from politics. In this delicate situation the intervention of the United States was precipitated by certain startling events. The incident created by the surreptitious publication of the letter of Señor Dupuy de Lome, Spanish minister at Washington, to Señor Canalejas, in which President McKinley was aspersed and the reciprocity negotiations between the two countries were exhibited as a sham, had just been officially declared to be closed, when the U. S. S. *Maine* was blown up at Havana, and two hundred and sixty-six of her crew perished. Superficial reasoners have wished to treat the destruction of the *Maine* as the justification and the cause of the intervention of the United States. The government of the United States, however, did not itself take that ground. It is true that the case of the *Maine* is mentioned in the preamble to the joint resolution of Congress, by which the intervention of the United States was authorized; but it is recited merely as the culmination of "abhorrent conditions," which had existed for more than three years. The destruction of the *Maine* doubtless kindled the intense popular feeling without which wars are seldom entered upon; but the government of the United States never charged—on the contrary, it refrained from charging—that the catastrophe was to be attributed to "the direct act of a Spanish official." Its intervention rested upon the ground that there existed in Cuba conditions so injurious to the United States, as a neighboring nation, that they could no longer be endured. Its action was analogous to what is known in private law as the abatement of a nuisance. On this ground the intervention was justified by the late Alphonse Rivier, one of the most eminent publicists in Europe, and on this ground its justification must continue to rest.

Any exposition of the American doctrine of nonintervention would be incomplete that failed specially to notice the rule of the United States with regard to the recognition of new governments—a rule which is indeed a corollary of that doctrine. In Europe, governments had been treated as legitimate or illegitimate, according to what was conceived to be the regularity or the irregularity of the succession of their rulers. The attitude of the United States on this question was early defined, when the National Convention in France proclaimed a republic. On that occasion Jefferson, as Secretary of State, in a letter to Gouverneur Morris, of March 12, 1793, which has become a classic, said: "We surely cannot deny to any nation that right whereon our own government is founded, that everyone may govern itself according to whatever form it pleases, and change these forms at its own will; and that it may transact its business with foreign nations through whatever organ it thinks proper, whether king, convention, assembly, committee, president, or anything else it may choose. The will of the nation is the only thing essential to be regarded." In a word, the United States maintained that the true test of a government's title to recognition is not the theoretical legitimacy of its origin, but the fact of its existence as the apparent exponent of the popular will. And from this principle, which is now universally accepted, it necessarily follows that recognition can regularly be accorded only when the new government has demonstrated its ability to exist. Recognition extended at an earlier stage of the revolution savors of an act of intervention, and as such must be defended on its merits, as is clearly set forth in President Roosevelt's message of January 4, 1904, in relation to the recognition of the Republic of Panama.

In connection with the principle of non-intervention, a prominent place must be given to the Monroe Doctrine, the object of which was to render intervention unnecessary by precluding the occasions for it. On September 26, 1815, the Emperors of Austria and Russia, and the King of Prussia, signed at Paris a personal league commonly called the Holy Alliance, the design of which was declared to be the administration of government, in matters both internal and external, according to the precepts of justice, charity and peace. To this end the allied monarchs, "looking upon themselves as delegated by Providence" to rule over their respective countries, engaged to "lend one another, on every occasion and in every place, assistance, aid, and support." In the course of time, as revolt against the arrangements of the Congress of Vienna spread and grew more pronounced, the alliance came more and more to assume the form of a league for the protection of the principle of legitimacy—the principle of the divine right of kings as opposed to the rights of the people—against the encroachments of liberal ideas. Congresses were held at Aix-la-Chapelle, Troppau and Laybach, for the purpose of maturing a programme to that end. The league was joined by the King of France; but England, whose Prince Regent had originally given it his informal adhesion, began to grow hostile. Her own government, with its free and parliamentary institutions, was founded on a revolution; and the allies, in the circular issued at Troppau, had associated "revolt and crime," and had declared that the European powers "had an undoubted right to take a hostile attitude in regard to those states in which the overthrow of the government might operate as an example." In a circular issued at Laybach they denounced "as equally null, and disallowed by the public law of Europe, any pretended reform effected by revolt and open force." In October, 1822, they held a congress at Verona for the purpose of concerting measures against the revolutionary government in Spain; and in yet another circular announced their determination "to repel the maxim of rebellion, in whatever place and under whatever form it might show itself." Their ultimate object was more explicitly stated in a secret treaty in which they engaged mutually "to put an end to the system of representative governments" in Europe, and to adopt measures to destroy "the liberty of the press." Popular movements were forcibly suppressed in Piedmont and Naples; and in April, 1823, France, acting for the allies, invaded Spain, for the purpose of restoring

the absolute monarch Ferdinand VII. Before th
close of the summer such progress had been mad
in this direction that notice was given to the Brit
ish government of the intention of the allies to cal
a congress with a view to the termination of th
revolutionary governments in Spanish America
At this time Lord Castlereagh, who had always bee
favorably disposed towards the alliance, had bee
succeeded in the conduct of the foreign affairs c
England by George Canning, who reflected th
popular sentiment as to the policy of the allie
powers. The independence of the Spanish-Amer
ican governments, which had now been acknowl
edged by the United States, had not as yet bee
recognized by Great Britain. But English mer
chants, like those of the United States, had devel
oped a large trade with the Spanish - America
countries, a trade which the restoration of thos
regions to a colonial condition would, under th
commercial system then in vogue, have cut off an
destroyed.

In view of this common interest, Canning, in th
summer of 1823, began to sound Richard Rush
the American minister at London, as to the pos
sibility of a joint declaration by the two goverr
ments against the intervention of the allies in Spar
ish America. Canning once boasted that he ha
called into being the New World to redress th
balance of the Old. The meaning of this boas

can be understood only in the light of his proposals. In a "private and confidential" note to Rush, of August 23, 1823, he declared: " 1. We conceive the recovery of the colonies by Spain to be hopeless. 2. We conceive the question of the recognition of them, as independent states, to be one of time and circumstances. 3. We are, however, by no means disposed to throw any impediment in the way of an arrangement between them and the mother-country by amicable negotiation. 4. We aim not at the possession of any portion of them ourselves. 5. We could not see any portion of them transferred to any other power with indifference." If these opinions and feelings were shared by the United States, Canning thought that the two governments should declare them in the face of the world, as the best means of defeating the project, if any European power should cherish it, of subjugating the colonies in the name of Spain, or of acquiring any part of them itself by cession or by conquest. He therefore desired Rush to act upon his proposals at once, if he possessed the power to do so. It was said of Richard Rush by an eminent Senator that, in the course of an unusually long and important diplomatic career, he "never said a word that was improper, nor betrayed a thought that might peril his country's fortunes." On the present occasion, he acted with his usual good judgment. His powers did not embrace the making of such a declaration as Canning desired; but, while he expressed the opinion that Canning's sentiments, except as to independence, which the United States had already acknowledged, were shared by his government, he lost no time in reporting the matter to the President. Monroe, on receiving the correspondence, hastened to take counsel upon it. Jefferson, whose opinion was solicited, replied: "Our first and fundamental maxim should be never to entangle ourselves in the broils of Europe; our second, never to suffer Europe to intermeddle with cis-Atlantic affairs." He was disposed to look with favor upon co-operation with England in the direction suggested. Madison shared his opinion. In the cabinet of Monroe, Calhoun inclined to invest Rush with power to join England in a declaration, even if it should pledge the United States not to take either Cuba or Texas. The President at first inclined to Calhoun's idea of giving Rush discretionary powers, but this was opposed by John Quincy Adams, who maintained that we could act with England only on the basis of the acknowledged independence of the Spanish-American states. The views of Adams prevailed. His basal thought was the right of self-government, which he believed it to be the duty and the interest of the United States to cherish and support. He thought that the United States should let England make her own declaration. This England did, without waiting

RICHARD RUSH

for the decision of the United States. On October 9, 1823, Canning, in an interview with Prince de Polignac, French ambassador, declared that while Great Britain would remain "neutral" in any war between Spain and her colonies, the "junction" of any foreign power with Spain against the colonies would be viewed as constituting "entirely a new question," upon which Great Britain "must take such decision" as her interests "might require."

In his annual message to Congress of December 2, 1823, President Monroe devoted to the subject a long passage. The substance of it is, however, conveyed in a few sentences. After adverting to the abstention of the United States from European wars and to the dangers to be apprehended from the system of the allied powers, he declared: "We owe it, therefore, to candor and to the amicable relations existing between the United States and those powers, to declare that we should consider any attempt on their part to extend their system to any portion of this hemisphere as dangerous to our peace and safety. With the existing colonies or dependencies of any European power, we have not interfered and shall not interfere. But with the governments who have declared their independence and maintained it, and whose independence we have, on great consideration and on just principles, acknowledged, we could not view any interposition for the purpose of oppressing them, or controlling in any other manner their destiny, by any European power, in any other light than a manifestation of an unfriendly disposition towards the United States."

The sentences just quoted specially relate to the aims of the Holy Alliance; but there is another passage in the message which is also often cited as embodying the Monroe Doctrine. In 1821 the Emperor of Russia, as we have seen, issued a ukase, by which he assumed, as owner of the shore, to exclude foreigners from carrying on commerce and from navigating and fishing within a hundred Italian miles of the northwest coast of America, from Bering Straits down to the fifty-first parallel of north latitude. As this assertion of title embraced territory which was claimed by the United States as well as by Great Britain, both those governments protested against it, as well as against the exorbitant jurisdictional pretension with which it was associated. In consequence the Russian government proposed to adjust the matter by amicable negotiation; and instructions to that end were prepared by John Quincy Adams for the American ministers at London and St. Petersburg. At a meeting of the cabinet on June 28, 1823, while the subject was under discussion, Adams expressed the opinion that the claim of the Russians could not be admitted, because they appeared to have no "settlement" upon the territory in dispute; and on

July 17 he informed Baron Tuyl, then Russian minister at Washington, "that we [the United States] should contest the right of Russia to any territorial establishment on this continent, and that we should assume distinctly the principle that the American continents are no longer subjects for *any* new European colonial establishments." With reference to this subject, President Monroe, in the message above quoted, said: "In the discussions to which this interest has given rise, and in the arrangements by which they may terminate, the occasion has been judged proper for asserting as a principle in which the rights and interests of the United States are involved, that the American continents, by the free and independent condition which they have assumed and maintain, are henceforth not to be considered as subjects for future colonization by any European powers."

By the term "future colonization," President Monroe evidently intended to convey the same meaning as was expressed by the terms "settlement" and "colonial establishments" previously employed by Adams. They were used to denote, what they were then commonly understood to mean, the acquisition of title to territory by original occupation and settlement. But in the course of time the phrase "future colonization" came to receive a broader interpretation. President Polk, in his annual message of December 2, 1845, declared that, while existing rights of every European nation should be respected, it should be "distinctly announced to the world as our settled policy, that no future European colony or dominion shall, with our consent, be planted or established on any part of the North American continent." By pronouncing against the establishment by a European power of any "dominion"—a term which included even the voluntary transfer of territory already occupied—President Polk expressed a conception which has come generally to prevail, and which is embodied in the popular phrase: "No more European colonies on these continents." The same meaning is conveyed in the phrase—"America for the Americans," which signifies that no European power shall be permitted to acquire new territory or to extend its dominions in the Western Hemisphere.

In this sense, but apparently with the qualification in the particular case that only a forcible acquisition of territory was forbidden, the Monroe Doctrine was invoked by President Cleveland in respect of the Venezuelan boundary question. This incident, as is well known, grew out of a long-standing dispute between Great Britain and Venezuela, which was the continuation of a dispute two centuries old between the Netherlands and Spain as to the limits of the Dutch and Spanish settlements in Guiana. In 1844 Lord Aberdeen proposed to Venezuela a conventional line, beginning at the river Moroco. This proposal was declined; and, chiefly in consequence of civil commotions in Venezuela, negotiations remained practically in abeyance till 1876. Venezuela then offered to accept the Aberdeen line; but Lord Granville suggested a boundary farther west; and in subsequent negotiations the British demand was extended still farther in that direction. Venezuela, representing that this apparent enlargement of British dominion constituted a pure aggression on her territorial rights, invoked the aid of the United States on the ground of the Monroe Doctrine. Venezuela asked for arbitration, and in so doing included in her claim a large portion of British Guiana. Great Britain at length declined to arbitrate unless Venezuela would first yield all territory within a line westward of that offered by Lord Aberdeen. In these circumstances, Mr. Olney, as Secretary of State, in instructions to Mr. Bayard, American ambassador at London, of July 20, 1895, categorically inquired whether the British government would submit the whole controversy to arbitration. In these instructions Mr. Olney declared that the Monroe Doctrine did not establish a "protectorate" over other American states; that it did not relieve any of them "from its obligations as fixed by international law nor prevent any European power directly interested from enforcing such obligations or from inflicting merited punishment for the breach of them"; but that its "single purpose and object" was that "no European power or combination of European powers" should "forcibly deprive an American state of the right and power of self-government and of shaping for itself its own political fortunes and destinies." This principle he conceived to be at stake in the dispute between Great Britain and Venezuela, because, as the dispute related to territory, it necessarily imported "political control to be lost by one party and gained by the other." "To-day," declared Mr. Olney, "the United States is practically sovereign on this continent, and its fiat is law upon the subjects to which it confines its interposition." All the advantages of this superiority were, he affirmed, at once imperilled if the principle should be admitted that European powers might convert American states into colonies or provinces of their own. Lord Salisbury declined unrestricted arbitration; and, when his answer was received, President Cleveland, on December 17, 1895, laid the correspondence before Congress. "If a European power, by an extension of its boundaries, takes possession of the territory of one of our neighboring republics against its will and in derogation of its rights," it was, said President Cleveland, the precise thing which President Monroe had declared to be "dangerous to our peace and safety"; but he added that "any adjustment of the boundary which that country [Venezuela] may deem for her advantage and may enter into of her own free will cannot of course be objected to by the United States." He then recommended the appointment by the United States of a commission to investigate the merits of the controversy, and declared that, if the title to the disputed territory should be found to belong to Venezuela, it would be the duty of the United States "to resist by every means in its power, as a wilful aggression upon its rights and interests, the appropriation by Great Britain of any lands or the exercise of governmental jurisdiction over any territory which, after investigation, we have determined of right belongs to Venezuela." This declaration produced great excitement, in the United States as well as in England. So far as it seemed to imply, as the language has often been construed to do, that the United States possessed the right, by means of an *ex parte* commission, appointed by itself and composed of its own citizens, authoritatively to fix the boundary between two other independent nations, it went beyond the immediate necessities of the case. If the commission had ever reported, it is probable that its conclusions, which conceivably might not have been entirely acceptable either to Great Britain or to Venezuela, would have been treated as advisory rather than definitive, and would have been made the basis of further correspondence with both those governments. The actual position intended to be insisted upon, as appears by Mr. Olney's instructions to Mr. Bayard, as well as the rest of President Cleveland's message, was that the United States would resist the palpable and substantial encroachment upon and appropriation by Great Britain of Venezuelan territory. This position was quite in harmony with the spirit of the Monroe Doctrine. Congress unanimously provided for the appointment of a commission of investigation; but the commission, immediately after its organization, addressed to Mr. Olney, through its president, Mr. Justice Brewer, a letter setting forth its peaceful and non-partisan character and the desirability of securing the co-operation of Great Britain and Venezuela in obtaining evidence. At the close of his letter, Mr. Justice Brewer observed: "The purposes of the pending investigation are certainly hostile to none, nor can it be of advantage to any that the machinery devised by the government of the United States to secure the desired information should fail of its purpose." This statement was communicated to Great Britain as well as to Venezuela, and both governments promptly responded to the appeal. The labors of the commission were, however, brought to a close by the conclusion of a treaty of arbitration, signed by Great Britain and Venezuela, but negotiated between Great Britain and the United States, the predominant feature of which was the application of the principle of prescription, under the definite rule that fifty years' adverse holding of a district, either by exclusive political control or by actual settlement, should suffice to constitute national title. The adoption of the principle of prescription, on which the arbitrators would necessarily have acted, even if it had not been incorporated into the treaty, at once rendered nugatory the greater part of the Venezuelan claim. Although the extreme British claim was not allowed, the territorial results of the arbitration were decidedly favorable to that government. It must, however, be conceded that the most important political result of the Venezuelan incident was not the decision upon the territorial question, but the official adoption of the Monroe Doctrine by the Congress of the United States, and its explicit acceptance by the principal maritime power of Europe.

An official exposition of the Monroe Doctrine was given by President Roosevelt in his annual message of December 3, 1901, in which he said: "The Monroe Doctrine is a declaration that there must be no territorial aggrandizement by any non-American power at the expense of any American power on American soil. It is in no wise intended as hostile to any nation in the Old World. . . . This doctrine has nothing to do with the commercial relations of any American power, save that it in truth allows each of them to form such as it desires. . . . We do not guarantee any state against punishment if it misconducts itself, provided that punishment does not take the form of the acquisition of territory by any non-American power." An occasion for the practical application of this definition soon arose. On December 11, 1901, the German ambassador at Washington left at the Department of State a memorandum in which it was stated that the German government proposed to take certain coercive measures against Venezuela for the satisfaction of claims, based partly on breaches of contract and partly on violent wrongs, which it had been found to be impracticable otherwise to bring to a settlement. At the same time the memorandum declared that "under no circumstances" would the German government consider in its proceedings "the acquisition or the permanent occupation of Venezuelan territory." In acknowledging the receipt of this memorandum, on December 16th, Mr. Hay adverted to the fact that the German ambassador, on his then recent return from Berlin, had conveyed personally to the President, and had afterwards repeated to himself, the assurance of the German Emperor that the imperial government had no purpose or intention to make even the smallest acquisition of territory on the South American continent or the adjacent islands; and in view of this circumstance, and of the further assurance given in the memorandum, Mr. Hay declared that the President, while "appreciating the courtesy of the German government in making him acquainted with

JOHN HAY

the state of affairs referred to," did not regard himself "as called upon to enter into the consideration of the claims in question." The coercive measures contemplated by the German government were postponed for a year, and were then taken in conjunction with the British government, which also made to the United States, on November 13, 1902, a frank communication of its purposes. To this communication Mr. Hay replied that the government of the United States, although it "regretted that European powers should use force against Central and South American governments, could not object to their taking steps to obtain redress for injuries suffered by their subjects, provided that no acquisition of territory was contemplated." In the hostilities with Venezuela that ensued, the assurances of the powers were honorably kept, but peaceful relations were eventually restored through the frank exercise of the friendly offices of the United States.

In popular discussions the position has sometimes been urged that it is a violation of the Monroe Doctrine for a European power to employ force against an American republic for the purpose of collecting a debt or satisfying a pecuniary demand, no matter what may have been its origin. For this supposition, which is discredited by the declarations and acts of President Roosevelt and Mr. Hay, there appears to be no official sanction. It is true that in Wharton's

International Law Digest, under the head of the "Monroe Doctrine," two alleged manuscript instructions of Mr. Blaine to the American minister at Paris, of July 23 and December 16, 1881, are cited as authority for the statement that "the government of the United States would regard with grave anxiety an attempt on the part of France to force by hostile pressure the payment by Venezuela of her debt to French citizens." The citation, however, is wholly inadvertent. Both instructions are published in the volume of *Foreign Relations* for 1881; and they refer, not to "hostile pressure," but to a rumored design on the part of France of "taking forcible possession of some of the harbors and a portion of the territory of Venezuela in compensation for debts due to citizens of the French Republic." Even in regard to this they nowhere express "grave anxiety," but merely argue that such a proceeding would be unjust to other creditors, including the United States, since it would deprive them of a part of their security; while they avow the "solicitude" of the government of the United States "for the higher object of averting hostilities between two republics for each of which it feels the most sincere and enduring friendship." In 1861 the government of the United States admitted the right of France, Spain, and Great Britain to proceed jointly against Mexico for the satisfaction of claims. "France," said Mr. Seward on that occasion, in an instruction to the American minister at Paris, of June 26, 1862, "has a right to make war against Mexico, and to determine for herself the cause. We have the right and interest to insist that France shall not improve the war she makes to raise up an anti-republican or anti-American government, or to maintain such a government there." In a similar vein, Mr. Seward, writing to the American minister in Chile, on June 2, 1866, with reference to the hostilities then in progress between Spain and the republics on the west coast of South America, and particularly to the bombardment of Valparaiso by the Spanish fleet, declared that the United States did not intervene in wars between European and American states "if they are not pushed, like the French war in Mexico, to the political point"; that the United States had "no armies for the purpose of aggressive war; no ambition for the character of a regulator."

A tendency is often exhibited to attach decisive importance to particular phrases in President Monroe's message of 1823, or to the special circumstances in which it originated, as if they furnished a definitive test of what should be done and what should be omitted under all contingencies. The verbal literalist would, on the one hand, make the United States an involuntary party to all controversies between European and American governments, in order that the latter may not be "oppressed";

while the historical literalist would, on the other hand, treat Monroe's declarations as obsolete, since the conditions to which they specially referred no longer exist. But, when we consider the mutations in the world's affairs, these modes of reasoning must be confessed to be highly unsatisfactory. The "Monroe Doctrine" has in reality become a convenient title by which is denoted a principle that doubtless would have been wrought out if the message of 1823 had never been written—the principle of the limitation of European power and influence in the Western Hemisphere. We have seen, in the first paper in this series, that, as early as 1778, the Continental Congress, in the treaty of alliance with France, obtained from its ally the renunciation of any claim to the British possessions in North America. When Washington, in his Farewell Address, observed that Europe had "a set of primary interests, which to us have none, or a very remote relation," he lent emphasis to the thought that it was desirable so far as possible to dissociate America from the vicissitudes of European politics. Giving to this thought a further reach, Jefferson, while President, in 1808, declared: "We shall be satisfied to see Cuba and Mexico remain in their present dependence; but very unwilling to see them in that of either France or England, politically or commercially. We consider their interests and ours as the same, and the object of both must be to exclude European influence from this hemisphere." On January 15, 1811, twelve years before Monroe's message was published, Congress, in secret session, "taking into view the peculiar situation of Spain and her American provinces," and "the influence which the destiny of the territory adjoining the southern border of the United States might have upon their security, tranquillity, and commerce," resolved that the United States could not "without serious inquietude, see any part of said territory pass into the hands of any foreign power"; and the President was authorized to occupy all or any part of the Floridas, "in the event of an attempt to occupy the same, or any part thereof, by any foreign government." These incidents and avowals, although they detract nothing from the force of Monroe's declarations, with which they are indeed in entire harmony, point to the rational conclusion that those declarations are to be considered rather as an important expression than as the exclusive and final test of American policy. In the long struggle, which was eventually crowned with success, to exclude European domination from the interoceanic canal routes, and to secure the construction of a neutralized canal under American auspices, American statesmen no doubt were aided by the authority of Monroe's declarations, but were by no means dependent upon them. It is a remarkable fact that Seward, neither in the formal demand

upon France in 1865 to desist from armed intervention in Mexico for the purpose of overthrowing
the domestic republican government under Juarez
and establishing on its ruins the foreign imperial
government under Maximilian, nor in any of the
official correspondence relating to the subject,
mentioned the Monroe Doctrine, although his
action came within the letter as well as the spirit
of the message of 1823. President Polk, on the
other hand, in pronouncing against the acquisition
of new dominion in North America by a European power, although he was well within the limits
of the Monroe Doctrine as it is now understood,
invoked a passage that fell far short of sustaining
his position. It would be easy to cite many similar
examples.

The Monroe Doctrine, as a limitation upon the
extension of European power and influence on the
American continents, is now generally recognized
as a principle of American policy. To its explicit
acceptance by Great Britain and Germany, there
may be added the declaration which was spread by
unanimous consent upon the minutes of The Hague
Conference, and which was permitted to be annexed
to the signature of the American delegates to the
convention for the peaceful adjustment of international disputes, that nothing therein contained
should be so construed as to require the United
States "to depart from its traditional policy of not

WILLIAM H. SEWARD

entering upon, interfering with, or entangling itself in the political questions or internal administration of any foreign state," or to relinquish " its traditional attitude toward purely American questions."

The latest application of the Monroe Doctrine is that which President Roosevelt has made in the case of Santo Domingo. In a letter read in New York, in May, 1904, at a dinner held to celebrate the anniversary of Cuban independence, he said: " Any country whose people conduct themselves well can count upon our hearty friendliness. If a nation shows that it knows how to act with decency in industrial and political matters; if it keeps order and pays its obligations, then it need fear no interference from the United States. Brutal wrong-doing, or impotence which results in the general loosening of the ties of civilized society, may finally require intervention by some civilized nation, and in the Western Hemisphere the United States cannot ignore its duty." These declarations President Roosevelt repeated, with only slight changes in phraseology, in his annual message to Congress in the following December. On February 15, 1905, he transmitted to the Senate, for its advice and consent, a treaty concluded at Santo Domingo City on the 7th of the same month, under which the United States agreed to undertake the adjustment of all Dominican debts, foreign and domestic, and to that end to take charge of and administer the custom-houses. In the message accompanying the treaty, President Roosevelt stated that conditions in Santo Domingo had for many years been growing steadily worse, that there had been many disturbances and revolutions, and that debts had been contracted beyond the power of the republic to pay. Those who profited by the Monroe Doctrine must, he affirmed, accept certain responsibilities along with the rights which it conferred; and the justification for assuming the responsibility proposed in the present instance was to be found in the fact that it was incompatible with international equity for the United States to refuse to allow other powers to take the only means at their disposal of satisfying the claims of their citizens and yet to refuse itself to take any such steps. Under the Monroe Doctrine the United States could not, said President Roosevelt, see any European power "seize and permanently occupy" the territory of an American republic, and yet such seizure might eventually offer the only way in which such a power could collect any debts, unless the United States should interfere. Under such circumstances the United States should take charge of the custom-houses. In the course of his message he further said: "Either we must abandon our duty under our traditional policy towards the Dominican people, who aspire to a republican form of government while they are actually drifting into a condition of permanent anarchy, in which case we must permit some other government to adopt its own measures in order to safeguard its own interests, or else we must ourselves take seasonable and appropriate action." And in conclusion he avowed the belief that the proposed treaty afforded a "practical test of the efficiency of the United States government in maintaining the Monroe Doctrine." The Senate adjourned without taking a vote on the treaty, final action on which was thus deferred. Meanwhile, under a *modus vivendi* concluded by President Roosevelt, an American citizen designated by him has been placed by the Dominican government in charge of the collection of the revenues, a certain proportion of which is to be deposited in a bank in New York, on account of the claims of creditors, till the question of ratification of the treaty shall be definitely determined.

VII

THE DOCTRINE OF EXPATRIATION

The Declaration of Independence enumerates as
among the "inalienable rights" with which "all
men" are "endowed by their Creator," "life, liberty,
and the pursuit of happiness." It has often been
remarked that this dogma, like the associated affirmation that "all men are created equal," was
evidently considered as an abstraction, since its
announcement was not conceived to render inad-
missible the continued holding in bondage of a large
servile population. This criticism, however, cannot,
certainly in its more sinister sense, be accepted as
just. All general declarations of human rights to a
large extent represent aspirations, for the perfect ful-
filment of which conditions altogether ideal would
be requisite. So long as human conditions are imperfect, the realization of the highest human aspirations will be imperfect. Even admitting, therefore, that the enumerated rights belonged to "all
men" and were "inalienable," there yet remained
the task of determining what they actually included
and what were their practical limitations. No

argument, beyond the common experience of daily life, was needed to demonstrate that the unregulated pursuit by each individual of his own will was incompatible with the existence of social order; and it was therefore freely conceded, even by the most extreme proponents of the theory of natural rights, that men, when living in society, must be considered as having yielded up a part of those rights for the sake of the common welfare. But the question still remained, to what extent had this been done?

We are now concerned with the answer to this question in only one particular. Does the right to "liberty" and the "pursuit of happiness," in the sense in which they may be called "inalienable," embrace, incidentally, a right on the part of the individual to expatriate himself at will? This was a question that was destined, in the growth and development of American policy, to give rise to important international controversies, some of which yet remain unadjusted. In order to grasp the meaning of these controversies, it is necessary at the outset clearly to understand just what was the point at issue. The word expatriation is often employed to denote merely the giving up of one's country, and more particularly one's native country, by a permanent change of abode; but, as used in diplomatic discussions, it signifies the change both of home and of allegiance, and more especially of allegiance. By the laws of all civilized countries, provision is made for the admission of aliens to citizenship. The process by which this is done is called naturalization. What is the effect of this process? Does it confer upon the individual a new political character, without divesting him of that which he previously had, thus exposing him, unless his original sovereign consent to the change, to the conflicting claims of a dual allegiance? or does it of its own force not only invest him with a new allegiance, but also free him from the obligations of the old? By the laws of the United States the alien was required, at the time of his admission to citizenship, to forswear all allegiance to his former sovereign; and no inquiry was made as to whether that sovereign had, either by general or by specific permission, consented to the act. It might therefore be inferred that they were framed upon the theory that the individual possessed an absolute and unrestricted right to change his allegiance, without regard to the claims which his country of origin might assert, even within its own jurisdiction. This would, however, be a hasty inference, so far, at any rate, as the omission to inquire concerning the claims of prior allegiance is concerned. Other countries had naturalization statutes, by which no such inquiry was authorized; and yet those countries conceded to their own subjects the right of expatriation only with substantial qualifications or not at all. While they granted naturalization, they did not claim that it dissolved the ties of prior allegiance and made its recipient an alien to his native country, without regard to the latter's laws on the subject. And we shall see that a long time elapsed before the United States advanced to the full assertion of this position in its diplomatic correspondence, and a still longer time before it embodied the claim in its legislation.

Nor is this surprising. The courts, and the most authoritative jurists, repeatedly expressed the opinion that the United States had inherited, as part of the common law, the English doctrine with regard to the change of allegiance. Chancellor Kent, reviewing in his *Commentaries* the decisions of the American courts, said that "the better opinion would seem to be, that a citizen cannot renounce his allegiance to the United States without the permission of government, to be declared by law," and that, as there was "no existing legislative regulation" on the subject, "the rule of the English common law" remained "unaltered." Mr. Justice Story, delivering in a certain case the judgment of the Supreme Court, laid down the general rule that individuals could not, "by any act of their own, without the consent of the government, put off their allegiance and become aliens"; while, in his work on the *Conflict of Laws*, he declared that every nation had "an exclusive right to regulate persons and things within its own territory, according to its own sovereign will and public policy." To this general current of legal authority there was just one exception, and that was a decision rendered by the court of appeals of Kentucky, in 1839, a decision in which there seemed to breathe the free and untrammelled spirit of the West. In this case it was declared that expatriation might be "considered a practical and fundamental doctrine of America"; but the qualification was immediately added that "the political obligations of the citizen, and the interests of the Republic," might "forbid a renunciation of allegiance by his mere volition or declaration at any time, and under all circumstances," and that for this reason "the government, for the purpose of preventing abuse and securing public welfare," might "regulate the mode of expatriation." Even as thus qualified, Chancellor Kent expressed disapproval of the decision, and maintained not only that "the weight of American authority" was "in favor of the opposite doctrine," but also that the opposite doctrine was "founded . . . upon the most safe and reliable principles."

In the earlier diplomatic correspondence of the United States, we find no radical dissent from the views generally expressed by the courts. It is true that Jefferson, as Secretary of State, in a letter to Gouverneur Morris, minister to France, of August 16, 1793, said that citizens of the United States were "certainly free to divest themselves of that character by emigration and other acts manifesting their intention," and might "then become the subjects of another power" and be "free to do whatever the subject of that power may do"; but this was far from saying that other countries were obliged to act upon the same doctrine. John Marshall, as Secretary of State, a few years later, in commenting upon the effects of naturalization, observed that no nation had a right to question its validity, "unless it be one which may have a conflicting title to the person adopted."

It is constantly stated that the United States maintained the right of expatriation in its controversies with Great Britain concerning the impressment of seamen. This is true, but only in a very limited sense. Taking the dispute over impressment as a whole, it did not involve the crucial point of the later controversies as to expatriation. The burden of the complaint in regard to impressment, as defined in Madison's war message of June 1, 1812, was that Great Britain sought, under cover of belligerent right, to execute her municipal law of allegiance on board the ships of other countries on the high seas, where no laws could operate "but the law of nations, and the laws of the country to which the vessels belong." Precisely the same position was maintained by Webster in his correspondence with Lord Ashburton in 1842. Ships on the high seas are treated, for purposes of jurisdiction, as if they were part of the territory of the nation to which they belong. The complaint that the British government enforced the English law of allegiance on board American vessels on the high seas was manifestly a different thing from objecting to her enforcement of the same law within British jurisdiction.

A comprehensive examination of our unpublished diplomatic records enables me to say that the first Secretary of State to announce the doctrine of expatriation in its fullest extent—the doctrine that naturalization in the United States not only clothes the individual with a new allegiance but also absolves him from the obligations of the old—was James Buchanan. In an instruction to George Bancroft, then American minister in London, of December 18, 1848, Buchanan, referring to the duty of protecting American citizens, naturalized as well as native, said: "We can recognize no difference between the one and the other, nor can we permit this to be done by any foreign government, without protesting and remonstrating against it in the strongest terms. The subjects of other countries who from choice have abandoned their native land, and, accepting the invitation which our laws present, have emigrated to the United States and become American citizens, are entitled to the very same rights and privileges as if they had been born in the country.

JAMES BUCHANAN

To treat them in a different manner would be a violation of our plighted faith as well as our solemn duty." The same doctrine was asserted by Buchanan, in terms equally unequivocal, on prior occasions. As early as November 25, 1845, he informed an inquirer that the fact of his having become a citizen of the United States by naturalization entitled him "to the same protection from this government that a native citizen would receive."

Buchanan's innovation was not, however, accepted by any of his successors as Secretary of State till he himself became President. Webster, as Secretary of State under Fillmore, fully adopted the view expressed by the eminent American publicist, Wheaton, when minister to Prussia, that naturalization would entitle its recipient to protection everywhere but in his native country. Edward Everett, Webster's successor under Fillmore, held to the same opinion. Nor did any reversal of it take place when Pierce succeeded Fillmore, and that Democrat of Democrats, William L. Marcy, became Secretary of State. In an instruction to the American minister to Sardinia, of November 10, 1855, Marcy, while declaring that a naturalized citizen of the United States had all the rights of a native, went on to observe that the vindication of those rights could not require or authorize "an interference in his behalf with the fair application to him of the municipal laws of his native country when he voluntarily subjects himself to their control in the same manner and to the same extent as they would apply if he had never left that country. A different view of the duties of this government would," added Marcy, "be an invasion of the independence of nations, and could not fail to be productive of discord; it might, moreover, prove detrimental to the interests of the States of this Union."

Views similar to these were expressed by Caleb Cushing, Attorney-General under Pierce, in 1856, in an opinion which he gave upon a question propounded by the Bavarian minister at Berlin as to the law in the United States. The results of an examination of judicial decisions, both Federal and State, Cushing summarized thus: "Expatriation a general right, subject to regulation of time and circumstances according to public interests; and the requisite consent of the state presumed where not negatived by standing prohibitions." Subject to "the conditions thus indicated," and to "such others as the public interest might seem to Congress to require to be imposed," he thought that the right of expatriation existed and might be freely exercised by citizens of the United States. He took occasion, however, to observe that opinion on the subject in the United States had always been "a little colored . . . by necessary opposition to the assumption of Great Britain to uphold the doctrine of indefeasible allegiance, and in terms to prohibit expatriation. Hence," he continued, "we have been prone to regard it hastily as a question between kings and their subjects. It is not so. The true question is of the relation between the political society and its members, upon whatever hypothesis of right and in whatever form of organization that society may be constituted. The assumption of a natural right of emigration, without possible restriction in law, can be defended only by maintaining that each individual has all possible rights against the society and the society none with respect to the individual; that there is no social organization, but a mere anarchy of elements, each wholly independent of the other, and not otherwise consociated save than by their casual coexistence in the same territory."

A pronounced change in the tone and language of the government was now impending, and for reasons altogether intelligible. In March, 1857, Buchanan became President, and conditions were ripe for the further development of the position which he had taken as Secretary of State ten years before. For several decades after the formation of the government of the United States, the immigrant element of the population was comparatively unimportant. It is estimated that the whole number of immigrants from 1790 to 1820 was only about 250,000. During the twenties it continued to be small; but in the next decade it grew rapidly. In the year 1842 the number reached 100,000. In 1846 there began the movement due to the Irish famine; and this movement, combined with bad times in Germany, produced in 1854 the enormous maximum of 427,833, which was not again reached till after the Civil War. In 1860 the foreign-born population of the United States was 4,138,697. In 1870 it was 5,567,229. Immigrants and the children of immigrants had come to form a large percentage of the country's citizenship. Such a condition of things inevitably produced an effect on the policy of the United States, just as it must have done on the policy of any other government founded on popular suffrage. The foreign-born citizen who desired to revisit the country of his origin, represented an interest so wide-spread and so powerful that its wishes could not be disregarded, no matter what the courts and publicists, or even what Secretaries of State, had said.

As the largest immigration prior to 1857 was from Ireland and the German states, controversies as to allegiance most frequently arose in those quarters. By the law of England, a British subject could not put off his natural allegiance except by act of Parliament, and of such an act there was no record. The law in Germany was more liberal. A Prussian subject, for example, might lose his allegiance in various ways, one of which was by living ten years in a foreign land. But this did not suffice to prevent a collision, since the laws of the United States required for naturalization only a five years' residence, and sometimes less; and since, above all, in Prussia as well as in other European states, the discharge from allegiance was always subject to the performance of military duties, whether the individual had at the time of his emigration reached the age of actual service or not.

In 1859 the issue was broadly made. In February of that year a native of Hanover, named Christian Ernst, who had emigrated to the United States eight years before, at the age of nineteen, was admitted to citizenship; and in the following month he procured a passport and returned to Hanover on a visit. On arriving in his native village he was arrested and forced into the army. President Buchanan gave to the case his immediate personal attention, and submitted it to Judge Jeremiah S. Black, his Attorney-General, for an opinion. Judge Black's opinion bore the significant date of the 4th of July. He advised that it was the "natural right of every free person, who owes no debts and is not guilty of crime, to leave the country of his birth in good faith and for an honest purpose," and to throw off his natural allegiance and substitute another for it; that, although the common law of England denied this right, and "some of our own courts, misled by British authority, have expressed, though not very decisively, the same opinion," this was not to be taken as settling the question; that "natural reason and justice, writers of known wisdom," and "the practice of civilized nations" were "all opposed to the doctrine of perpetual allegiance," and that the United States was pledged to the right of expatriation and could not without perfidy repudiate it; that expatriation "includes not only *emigration* out of one's native country, but *naturalization* in the country adopted as a future residence"; that "naturalization does *ipso facto* place the native and the adopted citizen in precisely the same relations with the government under which they live, except in so far as the express and positive law of the country has made a distinction in favor of one or the other"; that there was no law in the United States that made any difference between native and naturalized citizens with regard to protection abroad; that the opinion held by "persons of very high reputation," that a naturalized citizen ought to be protected everywhere except in the country of his birth, had "no foundation to rest upon . . . except the dogma which denies altogether the right of expatriation without the consent of his native country"; that, even assuming that Hanover had a municipal regulation by which the right of expatriation was denied to those of her subjects who failed to comply with certain conditions, and that this regulation was violated by Ernst when he came away, the unlawfulness of his emigration would not make his naturalization

WILLIAM L. MARCY

void as against the King of Hanover; that, if the laws of the two countries were in conflict, the law of nations must decide the question upon principles and rules of its own; and that, "by the public law of the world we have the undoubted right to naturalize a foreigner, whether his natural sovereign consented to his emigration or not"; and, finally, that the government of Hanover could justify Ernst's arrest only by proving that the original right of expatriation depended upon the consent of the natural sovereign—a proposition which, said Judge Black, "I am sure no man can establish."

On July 8, 1859, the views of the President in relation to the case of Christian Ernst and analogous cases were communicated to Mr. Wright, American minister at Berlin, in a paper that at once acquired great celebrity. In this paper the views announced by Judge Black, which in reality were but a reiteration of those held by Buchanan as Secretary of State, were fully adopted. What right, it was asked, did the laws of the United States confer upon a foreigner by granting him naturalization? The answer was, all the rights, privileges, and immunities which belonged to a native citizen, except that of eligibility to the office of President. "With this exception," it was affirmed, "the naturalized citizen, from and after the date of his naturalization, both at home and abroad, is placed upon the very same footing with the native citizen. He is neither in a better nor a worse condition . . . The moment a foreigner becomes naturalized, his allegiance to his native country is severed forever. He experiences a new political birth. A broad and impassable line separates him from his native country. He is no more responsible for anything he may say or do, or omit to say or do, after assuming his new character than if he had been born in the United States. Should he return to his native country, he returns as an American citizen, and in no other character. In order to entitle his original government to punish him for an offence, this must have been committed while he was a subject and owed allegiance to that government." This instruction was signed by Mr. Cass, but in its citations of the law of Pennsylvania, as well as in its sentiments and style, it bears Presidential ear-marks. On August 20, 1859, the Hanoverian government stated that a "full pardon" had been granted to Ernst, and that he had been "dismissed" from the military service, but added that similar conflicts could be prevented in the future only by the United States "renouncing its own views on the subject, which did not agree with international relations," or by concluding a special arrangement. President Buchanan, however, in his annual message of December 3, 1860, declared: "Our government is bound to protect the rights of our naturalized citizens everywhere to the same extent as though they had drawn their first breath in this country. We recognize no distinction between our native and naturalized citizens."

The instruction to Mr. Wright was printed and issued by the Department of State in circular form, for the purpose of defining the position which the United States would in future maintain. It was so used by Seward, as Secretary of State, after Lincoln had succeeded Buchanan as President. But, as the Civil War grew more serious and the United States was forced to adopt a policy of conscription, Seward permitted the controversy to rest. Writing to Motley, who was then minister to Austria, on April 21, 1863, he adverted to the perplexities in which the United States had become involved by refusing, on the one hand, to exempt from its military service persons whom foreign powers claimed the right to protect, while demanding, on the other, the exemption of a like class from military service in the country of their origin on the ground of their having become citizens of the United States. The President had, he said, decided that it was not expedient in the crisis then existing to urge questions of the latter sort beyond the limits of an appeal to the good-will and friendly disposition of foreign powers. It was, besides, deemed necessary to discourage rather than encourage the return of naturalized foreigners to their native country, as well as the emigration of American citizens to Europe.

But, soon after the close of the war, Seward was

somewhat violently torn away from this position by the outbreak, in 1866, of the Fenian agitation, and the arrest in British jurisdiction of naturalized American citizens, natives of Ireland, for acts done in furtherance of that movement. Among the numerous cases of this kind, the most notable one, historically, was that of Warren and Costello, who were members of the discordant and ill-starred expedition on the brigantine *Jacmel* to the coast of Ireland, and who were afterwards tried and convicted at Dublin on a charge of treason-felony. At that time an alien charged with crime in British jurisdiction was by law entitled to be tried by what was technically called a jury *de medietate linguæ*— a jury composed half of British subjects and half of foreigners. Warren and Costello applied for such a jury, on the ground that they were American citizens. Had they been native citizens of the United States, their request would have been granted, but, as they were British subjects by birth, it was refused, the court citing Blackstone, Kent, and Story to show that their original allegiance still survived.

The trial and conviction of Warren and Costello, as well as of other prisoners, under these circumstances produced an excitement that, to borrow Seward's picturesque phrase, extended "throughout the whole country, from Portland to San Francisco and from St. Paul to Pensacola." Public meetings attended by immense crowds were held in many cities, and resolutions were adopted calling upon the government for vigorous measures. In this agitation the leading spirit was William E. Robinson, then a member of Congress from Brooklyn, popularly known as "Richelieu" Robinson, "Richelieu" being the name under which he practised journalism. Robinson was a native of Ireland and an advocate of her independence, or, as he once declared in Congress, of her purchase and annexation by the United States. When in the latter part of 1867 Congress assembled, he at once brought up the subject of the Irish-American prisoners. He offered resolutions of inquiry looking to the impeachment of the American minister at London, and of the American consul at Dublin, for neglect of duty; and declared that unless every American citizen then confined in a British jail, against whom a charge of crime had not already been filed, should not on demand be instantly released, the American minister should "come home and breathe his native air, and be prepared to stand up like a man, and not be trembling all over like a jelly." As the minister thus described was no other than Charles Francis Adams, who, in the dark hours of the great American conflict, could quietly say to Earl Russell, with reference to the apprehended escape of "Lairds' Ironclads," "It would be superfluous in me to point out to your lordship that this is war," it is obvious that Mr. Robinson was a man of fancy, though tastes will necessarily differ as to the quality of his wit. On a subsequent occasion he proposed a resolution, which was at once voted by the House of Representatives, requesting the President to obtain the release of Warren and Costello and "their return to our flag, with such ceremonies as are appropriate to the occasion." Warren and Costello were eventually released, but without special ceremonial incidents.

Meanwhile, the Committee on Foreign Affairs, spurred on by ninety-six resolutions and memorials that had been adopted at public meetings in different sections of the country, all demanding that action be taken to secure to citizens of the United States protection abroad, had been wrestling with various proposals designed to accomplish that end; and on January 27, 1868, the chairman, General Banks, brought in a bill, accompanied by an elaborate report. The report was both able and temperate. It pertinently declared that the claim of "indefeasible allegiance and perpetual service" was the symbol of "feudalism and force," but it also affirmed that "the law of allegiance and of service" was "as essential to a republic at it is to a monarchy," and that the "extinction of the mutual obligations between a government and its subject" should depend upon "the express or implied consent of both parties," under proper regulations. The bill was less carefully reasoned, and, after some discussion, was recommitted. It was reported again, in a form much altered, on March 10th. In its new form it declared that the "right of expatriation" was "a natural and inherent right of all people, indispensable to the enjoyment of the rights of life, liberty, and the pursuit of happiness," and that "any declaration, instruction, opinion, order, or decision," of any officer of the government, which denied, restricted, impaired, or questioned that right, was "inconsistent with the fundamental principles" of the government. It further provided that naturalized citizens of the United States should while abroad receive the same protection as native citizens in like circumstances; and empowered the President, whenever a citizen of the United States should be arrested and detained by a foreign government upon the allegation that naturalization in the United States did not operate to dissolve his original allegiance, to retaliate by arresting and detaining any subject of that government found within the national jurisdiction.

The bill, after discussion and amendment, passed the House on April 20, 1868, by a vote of 104 to 4, 81 members not voting. In the Senate it was referred to the Committee on Foreign Relations, from which it was reported by the chairman, Mr. Sumner, on June 23d, with two amendments, one of which struck out the provision for reprisals and made it the duty of the President, in cases of improper arrest and detention, merely to report the facts to Congress. In the debate that ensued, Mr. Williams, of Oregon, moved to substitute for this amendment a clause making it the duty of the President, before reporting the facts to Congress, to use all means, not amounting to acts of war, to obtain the prisoner's release. This amendment was eventually adopted. The bill, as amended, passed the Senate on July 25, 1868, by a vote of 39 to 5, 20 Senators not voting. On the same day the amendments of the Senate were concurred in by the House, and on July 27th the bill, with the approval of the President, became a law.

An examination of the debates shows that the passage of the bill was greatly facilitated by two circumstances, which were repeatedly mentioned. One was that, while the bill was pending, both the great political parties held their national conventions and adopted declarations in favor of the equal protection of all citizens, both native and naturalized, at all times and in all places. The other was that George Bancroft had, with the kindly and powerful co-operation of Bismarck, concluded on February 22, 1868, with the North German Union his epoch-making naturalization treaty, which was soon followed by similar treaties with Baden and Bavaria, and by the promise or well-founded expectation of treaties with yet other powers, including Great Britain. Indeed, the principles of a naturalization treaty with Great Britain were settled in a protocol signed in London as early as October 9, 1868, though they were not embodied in a formal convention till May 13, 1870, when Parliament had by an act of the preceding day adopted the necessary legislation. Before the close of 1872, naturalization treaties were made with Hesse (1868), Belgium (1868), Sweden and Norway (1869), Austria - Hungary (1870), Ecuador (1872), and Denmark (1872). Of all these treaties, however, that with Great Britain is the most liberal, since it recognizes the fullest possible effects of naturalization, whether American or British, whenever acquired, while all the rest make a five years' residence in the country of adoption a necessary condition of expatriation, even though naturalization should, as in some cases it may, be sooner obtained. The treaty with Great Britain is therefore the only one that meets the full exactions of the act of July 27, 1868; but they were all promptly ratified.

Since 1872 the government of the United States has earnestly and constantly striven to secure naturalization treaties with other powers, but its efforts have been rewarded only in the single and unimportant case of Hayti. For this failure there are several reasons, first among which we may mention the controversies that have arisen under the existing treaties, in consequence of the return to their native country, immediately after their naturalization in the United States, of young men who emigrated just before arriving at the age when they were subject to military duty. While the number of such persons from year to year has been comparatively small, yet it has, as the volumes of diplomatic correspondence amply testify, been large enough to produce incalculable mischief. This unfortunate complication, which has in some instances put in jeopardy subsisting arrangements, has naturally served as an obstacle to the formation of new ones. Besides, the increasing pressure of the military system in Europe has made the non-treaty powers more and more reluctant to recognize the expatriation of any citizen or subject who has not performed the entire military service which the law prescribes. This tendency is clearly seen in the case of France, who, abandoning a less stringent rule formerly applied, now enforces her military laws upon Frenchmen naturalized abroad who were at the time of their naturalization subject to military service in the active army or in the reserve of that army. By the Italian civil code of 1866, citizenship of that country is lost by naturalization abroad, but it is expressly declared by the same code that this does not carry with it exemption from the obligation of military service or from the penalties inflicted on those who bear arms against their native country. Other countries, including Switzerland, have laws of similar purport; but the Swiss laws contain a provision under which a native of that country may, if he sees fit to do so, renounce his natural allegiance. The most difficult case, however, to deal with is that of Russia, by whose laws any native of that country who enters a foreign service without the permission of his government, or takes the oath of allegiance to a foreign power, is exposed to the loss of all civil rights and perpetual banishment from the empire, or, in case of his unauthorized return to Russia, to deportation to Siberia. In addition to this, he is required to perform his term of military service. Turkey, prior to 1869, recognized the right of expatriation, but has since refused to do so. Referring to the situation thus created, President McKinley, in his annual message of December 5, 1899, said: "Our statutes do not allow this government to admit any distinction between the treatment of native and naturalized Americans abroad, so that ceaseless controversy arises in cases where persons, owing in the eye of international law a dual allegiance, are prevented from entering Turkey or are expelled after entrance. Our law in this regard contrasts with that of the European states. The British act, for instance, does not claim effect for the naturalization of an alien in the event of his return to his native country, unless the change be recognized by the law of that country or stipulated by treaty between it and the naturalizing state." It may be doubted whether this statement, so far as it relates to a "dual allegiance," was made with full appreciation of its significance; for if it be admitted that an alien naturalized in the United States, as a result owes, under international law, a dual allegiance, it necessarily follows that the doctrine of voluntary expatriation has no foundation in international law. No one has ever contended that the naturalization of an alien is ineffective in the country in which it is granted. The only question that has existed is as to its effect in other countries, and especially in the country of origin. The doctrine embodied in the act of 1868 is that naturalization invests the individual with a new and single allegiance, and by consequence absolves him from the obligations of the old. The position of governments and of publicists who deny the American contention is that naturalization merely adds a new allegiance to the old, so that the individual becomes subject to a dual allegiance, and may be held to all the obligations of his original citizenship if he returns to his native country. The doctrine of dual allegiance is, in a word, the precise test the acceptance of which distinguishes those who reject the doctrine of voluntary expatriation from those who support it.

But, quite apart from conditions existing in other countries, it would be uncandid not to admit that the failure of the United States since 1872 to extend the operation of the doctrine of expatriation may in a measure be ascribed to certain acts that have seemed to discredit the declarations made in the act of 1868. By the naturalization laws of the United States prior to 1870, admission to citizenship was restricted to "free white" persons. By the act of July 14, 1870, Congress, after the adoption of the Thirteenth and Fourteenth Amendments to the Constitution, changed the laws so as to embrace persons of "African" nativity or descent. While this act was under discussion in Congress, Senator Sumner made repeated efforts to strike from the laws the word "white," but in this he was unsuccessful. In the preparation of the Revised Statutes of the United States, the word "white" was omitted, but by the act of February 18, 1875, Congress corrected this omission by expressly restricting the right of naturalization to "white" persons and to persons of "African" nativity or descent. This legislation, under which Chinese, Japanese, and persons of various other races, being neither "white" nor "African," have been held to be incapable of naturalization in the United States, necessarily impaired the moral if not the legal authority of the act of 1868. The act of 1868 declared expatriation to be "a natural and inherent right of all people," and the right of expatriation, as correctly held by Judge Black, includes both emigration and naturalization. It is obvious therefore that the right of expatriation is only imperfectly recognized where people, not individually because of misconduct, but

in the mass because of their race, are excluded from
naturalization. Some of the very words of the act
of July 27, 1868, declaratory of the right of expatriation, were embodied on the following day in the
treaty with China, commonly called the Burlingame
treaty.

Any discussion of the subject of expatriation
would be incomplete which omitted to take notice
of the impression that has heretofore prevailed, and
may still widely prevail, that the United States has
on some occasions contended that a declaration of
intention to become a citizen clothed the individual
with American nationality and gave him the same
right to protection abroad as if he had been naturalized. This impression is altogether erroneous, and
is directly opposed to the positive declarations of a
long line of Secretaries of State, including Buchanan,
Marcy, Cass, Fish, Evarts, Frelinghuysen, Bayard,
Blaine, Olney, and Hay. In reality the statutes of
the United States forbid the issuance of passports
to persons who are not actual citizens. The erroneous impression with regard to the effect of a declaration of intention seems to be connected with the
particular case of Martin Koszta, in which William
L. Marcy is supposed to have maintained that by
such a declaration an alien acquired American nationality. Marcy, however, took no such ground.
The only purpose for which he referred to Koszta's
declaration of intention was that of showing that

Koszta was domiciled in the United States. He did maintain that a person's domicil, by which is meant his permanent home, may in certain relations invest him with a nationality. But even in this regard the position of Marcy has been much misapprehended. A brief explanation of the case will conduce to a clearer understanding of it.

Martin Koszta, a Hungarian by birth and an Austrian subject, was an active participant in the Hungarian revolution of 1848–49. At its close he, with many others, took refuge in Turkey. Their extradition was demanded by Austria but was resisted by Turkey, backed up by England and France; and they were at length released on the understanding that they would go into foreign parts. Many of them emigrated to the United States. Among these was Koszta, who, on July 31, 1852, declared his intention to become a citizen. Nearly two years later he temporarily returned, on private business, to Turkey, and placed himself under the protection of the American consul at Smyrna, by whom he was furnished with a tezkereh, a kind of passport or safe-conduct given by foreign consuls in Turkey to persons whom they assume to protect. While waiting for an opportunity to return to the United States, Koszta was seized and thrown into the sea, where he was picked up by a boat's crew, lying in wait for him, and taken on board the Austrian man-of-war *Huszar*, where he was confined in irons. It

afterwards transpired that his seizure was insti-
gated by the Austrian consul-general at Smyrna,
and that the Turkish officials had refused to grant
any authority for the purpose. The American consul at Smyrna and the American *chargé d'affaires*
at Constantinople sought to effect his liberation,
but in vain. Just then, however, the American
sloop-of-war *St. Louis* arrived at Smyrna, and her
commander, Captain Ingraham, after inquiring into
the circumstances of the case, demanded Koszta's
release, and intimated that he would resort to force
if the demand was not complied with by a certain
hour. An arrangement was then made by which
Koszta was delivered into the custody of the French
consul-general, until the United States and Austria
should agree as to the manner of disposing of him.

When a report of the transaction was received at
Washington, Marcy justified Captain Ingraham's
conduct, chiefly on the ground that Koszta, while
at Smyrna, had, according to the local custom,
which was recognized by international law, the right,
as a Frank or sojourner, to place himself under any
foreign protection that he might select; that he did
in fact place himself under the protection of the
American consul at Smyrna; and that, having thus
been clothed with the nationality of the protecting
power, he became entitled to be regarded while in
that situation as a citizen of the United States.
These views Marcy afterwards elaborated in his an-

swer to the protest lodged by Austria against Captain Ingraham's action. The links in Marcy's chain of reasoning, in this celebrated paper, were that, as the seizure and rescue of Koszta took place within the jurisdiction of a third power, the respective rights of the United States and of Austria, as parties to the controversy that had arisen concerning that transaction, could not be determined by the municipal law of either country, but must be determined by international law; that, as the previous political connection between Koszta and the Austrian government had, by reason of the circumstances of his emigration and banishment, been, even under the laws of Austria, dissolved, he could not at the time of his seizure be claimed as an Austrian subject, nor could his seizure as such be justified by Austria, either under international law or her treaties with Turkey; that the seizure in its method and circumstances constituted an outrage so palpable that any by-stander would have been justified, on elementary principles of justice and humanity, in interposing to prevent its consummation; that there were, however, special grounds on which the United States might, under international law—that being under the circumstances the only criterion — assert a right to protect Koszta; that, although he had ceased to be a subject of Austria, and had not become a citizen of the United States, and therefore could not claim the rights of a citizen under the municipal laws of either country, he might under international law derive a national character from domicil; that even if Koszta was not by reason of his domicil invested with the nationality of the United States, he undoubtedly possessed, under the usage prevailing in Turkey, which was recognized and sanctioned by international law, the nationality of the United States from the moment when he was placed under the protection of the American diplomatic and consular agents and received from them his tezkereh; that, as he was clothed with the nationality of the United States, and as the first aggressive act was committed by the procurement of the Austrian functionaries, Austria, if she upheld what was done, became in fact the first aggressor, and was not entitled to an apology for the measures adopted by Captain Ingraham to secure his release; that Captain Ingraham's action was further justified by the information which he received of a plot to remove Koszta clandestinely, in violation of the amicable arrangement under which he was to be retained at Smyrna while the question of his nationality was pending; and finally, that, as the seizure of Koszta was illegal and unjustifiable, the President could not consent to his delivery to the Austrian consul-general at Smyrna, but expected that measures would be taken to cause him to be restored to the condition he was in before he was seized.

THE DOCTRINE OF EXPATRIATION

On October 14, 1853, the American consul and the Austrian consul-general at Smyrna, acting under instructions from the American and Austrian ministers at Constantinople, requested the French consul-general to deliver Koszta over into the custody of the United States; and on the same day Koszta took passage on the bark *Sultana* for Boston.

VIII

ALTHOUGH the independence of the United States was won by the sword, the founders of the American Republic were accustomed to look upon war as a measure that could be justified only as a choice of evils. Standing armies and elaborate preparations for war they deprecated as a menace to liberty. Having proclaimed as the basis of their political system the consent of the governed, they cherished as their ideal a peaceful nation, always guided by reason and justice. In order that this ideal might be attained, they perceived the necessity of establishing international relations on definite and sure foundations. To that end they became ardent expounders of the law of nations; and their predilection for legal methods naturally found expression in the employment of arbitration for the settlement of international differences.

By arbitration we mean the determination of controversies by international tribunals judicial in their constitution and powers. Arbitration is not to be confounded with mediation. Mediation is an advisory, arbitration a judicial, process. Mediation recommends, arbitration decides. And while it may be true that nations have for this reason sometimes accepted mediation when they were unwilling or reluctant to arbitrate, yet it is also true that they have settled by arbitration questions which mediation could not have adjusted. It is, for instance, hardly conceivable that the question of the *Alabama* claims could have been settled by mediation. The same thing may be said of many boundary disputes. The importance of mediation, as one of the forms of amicable negotiation, should not, indeed, be minimized. A plan of mediation even may, as in the case of The Hague convention for the peaceful settlement of international disputes, form a useful auxiliary to a system of arbitration; but the fact should nevertheless be understood that the two processes are fundamentally different, and that, while mediation is only a form of diplomacy, arbitration consists in the application of law and of judicial methods to the determination of international disputes.

The government of the United States had been in existence only five years, when it found occasion to employ arbitration for the settlement of serious differences with the mother-country. Important provisions of the treaty of peace remained unexecuted. Various posts along the northern frontier were still held by the British forces, and the British government refused to evacuate them because of the failure of the United States to render effectual the engagement that British creditors should meet with no lawful impediment to the recovery of their confiscated debts. Moreover, almost immediately after the ratification of the treaty of peace, a question arose as to what was the "River St. Croix," which was to form the eastern boundary of the United States in its course northward from the Bay of Fundy. Such a river appeared on the map used by the negotiators of the treaty, but no stream answering to the name was afterwards found. The uncertainty as to the boundary was embarrassing, while the controversy as to the surrender of the posts and the recovery of debts formed a prolific source of irritation. But a still more acute cause of quarrel arose when, in 1793, the governments of France and Great Britain began to fulminate and enforce measures invasive of the rights of neutral trade. The situation then became so tense that, apparently as the only alternative to measures of force, Washington decided to send a special mission to England. John Jay, who was chosen for that delicate task, submitted his first formal representations to Lord Grenville on July 30, 1794. In the treaty concluded on the 19th of the following November, provision was made for three arbitrations. The first of these related to the boundary question; the second, to the claims on account of confiscated debts; the third, to the subject of neutral rights and duties.

The boundary question was referred to a mixed commission of three persons, which met at Halifax, Nova Scotia, on August 30, 1796, and rendered its award at Providence, Rhode Island, on October 25, 1798, holding that the Schoodiac, or Schoodic, was the river intended under the name of the St. Croix.

The claims of British subjects, on account of the impediments which they had encountered in their efforts to collect in the State courts their confiscated debts, were referred to a mixed commission of five persons, which met at Philadelphia in May, 1797. The proceedings of this body were inharmonious, and its sittings were suspended on July 31, 1798, by the withdrawal of the two American members. Differences of opinion on questions of law were to be expected, but the discussions at the board also developed personal feeling. This appears to have been largely due to the action of Mr. Macdonald, one of the British commissioners, a gentleman who no doubt deserved all the commendations bestowed upon him at the time of his appointment for rectitude and good-will, but who seems unfortunately to have possessed a sense of duty unmitigated by a sense of proportion. Wishing to be entirely candid with his associates, he made it a rule freely to acquaint them with all his opinions; and he adopted the practice of presenting to the board, when it was not otherwise occupied, memoranda expressive of his views. The final rupture was caused by his submitting a resolution which declared that from the beginning of the Revolution down to the treaty of peace the United States, whatever may have been their relation to other powers, stood to Great Britain in an attitude of rebellion. As it has always been the doctrine of the United States that the treaty of peace did not grant their independence, but merely recognized it as a condition existing from July 4, 1776, the date of its declaration, the American commissioners regarded the resolution as gratuitously offensive and withdrew. The claims which the commission failed to adjust were settled by a treaty concluded January 8, 1802, under which the British government accepted the sum of £600,-000 in satisfaction of its demands.

But the most important, as well as the most interesting, of the arbitral tribunals under the Jay treaty, was that which sat at London for the purpose of disposing of American claims against Great Britain on account of captures made under the orders in council, and of British claims against the United States on account of the latter's failure completely to enforce its neutrality. The membership of this board was worthy of the great questions submitted to its determination. The American commissioners were Christopher Gore, who, although popularly known as the legal preceptor of Daniel

Webster, achieved an eminence of his own; and William Pinkney, of Maryland, who, besides winning distinction in diplomacy and statesmanship, was the acknowledged leader of the American bar of his time. The British commissioners were Sir John Nicholl, an eminent civilian, who was afterwards succeeded by Maurice Swabey; and John Anstey. The fifth commissioner was Colonel John Trumbull, of Connecticut, who had accompanied Jay to England when he negotiated the treaty. The mode by which Trumbull was chosen is worthy of mention. The treaty provided that in case the four commissioners, two of whom were to be appointed by each government, could not agree upon the fifth, he should be chosen by lot. In execution of this stipulation, the commissioners on each side presented to the others a list of four persons; but, as neither side would yield, it became necessary to resort to the casting of lots. The next step, according to common practice, would have been for each side to place in the urn a name of its own independent selection, with the chances in favor of his being a partisan. But at London each side selected its name from the list of four made out by the other with a view to a mutual agreement, and the result was that a well-disposed man became the fifth commissioner.

The board had not been long in session when a serious controversy arose as to its power to determine its own jurisdiction in respect of the several claims presented for its decision. The division of opinion was so pronounced that for a time the British commissioners absented themselves from the meetings, but the difficulty was eventually submitted to Lord Chancellor Loughborough, who ended it by declaring "that the doubt respecting the authority of the commissioners to settle their own jurisdiction was absurd, and that they must necessarily decide upon cases being within or without their competency."

Important questions of law came before the commissioners in relation to contraband, the rights of neutrals, and the finality of the decisions of prize courts. These were all discussed with marked ability, especially by Pinkney. His opinions as a member of the board Wheaton justly pronounced to be "finished models of judicial eloquence, uniting powerful and comprehensive argument with a copious, pure, and energetic diction"; and they are almost all we possess in a complete and authentic form of the legal reasoning of the great master by whom they were delivered. The sessions of the board were brought to a close on February 24, 1804, all the business before it having been finished. There was, however, an interruption in its proceedings from July 30, 1799, to February 15, 1802, pending the diplomatic adjustment of the difficulty caused by the breaking up of the commission at Philadelphia.

WILLIAM PINKNEY

By reason of the fact that the proceedings of the London commission have only lately been published, its labors have not received from writers the attention which they deserve. It was estimated that, through the operation of the stipulation under which the commissioners sat, American claimants recovered from the British government the enormous sum of $11,650,000. "The whole of this sum," says Trumbull, "was promptly and punctually paid to each claimant, or his assignee; for, after a careful and accurate examination of the merits of every case of complaint, the awards of the board were made in favor of each individual, in the form of an order to pay, and payable at the treasury of Great Britain; nor do I recollect even to have heard a single complaint, of the delay of an hour, in any instance of an award presented for payment." The aggregate of the awards against the United States appears to have been $143,428.14; but although this amount was relatively small, its payment established the principle that a government is liable in damages for neglect to perform its neutral duties, and thus laid the foundation of the award made in 1872 at Geneva.

Since the close of the arbitral proceedings under the Jay treaty, arbitration has, except in the case of the extraordinary train of events that led up to the war of 1812, been almost habitually employed by the United States and Great Britain for the settlement of controversies that could not be adjusted by negotiation. Like the Jay treaty, the treaty of Ghent, of December 24, 1814, which restored peace between the two countries, provided for three arbitrations. The first related to the ownership of certain islands in Passamaquoddy Bay and the Bay of Fundy; the second, to the ascertainment of the boundary of the United States from the source of the river St. Croix to the river St. Lawrence; the third, to the determination of the boundary along the middle of the Great Lakes and of their water communications to the most northwestern point of the Lake of the Woods. In 1818, a difference as to the performance by Great Britain of her obligation under the treaty of Ghent, not to carry away from United States territory then in her possession "any slaves or other private property," was referred to the Emperor of Russia. He rendered a decision in favor of the United States, and in 1822 a mixed commission was erected in order to fix the amount to be paid. In 1827 a dispute as to the northeastern boundary was referred to the King of the Netherlands; but as his award was recommendatory rather than decisive, both governments agreed to waive it, and the question was settled by the Webster-Ashburton treaty. In 1853 a convention was entered into for the settlement by means of a mixed commission of all outstanding claims. The commission sat in London, and disposed of many important controversies, including the celebrated case of the *Creole*, which so nearly caused a rupture of relations in 1842. For the peculiarly satisfactory results of the board's labors, credit was perhaps chiefly due to the umpire, Joshua Bates, an American by birth, but then the head of the house of the Barings, who exhibited in his decisions the same broad intelligence and sound judgment as had characterized his exceptionally successful career in business. By the reciprocity treaty of 1854, by which the troubles as to the northeastern fisheries were temporarily allayed, arbitration was employed for the purpose of determining what fisheries were exclusively reserved to the inhabitants of the two countries under the agreement. In 1863 another arbitral board was erected for the purpose of deciding upon the claims of the Hudson's Bay Company and the Puget's Sound Agricultural Company against the United States for damages to their property and rights in connection with the treaty of 1846, by which the limits between the United States and the British possessions west of the Rocky Mountains were established.

This board was still in session when the relations between the United States and Great Britain were seriously disturbed by the controversies growing out of the civil war, the northeastern fisheries, and the disputed San Juan water boundary. These differences were all composed by the great treaty signed at Washington on May 8, 1871, on the part of the United States by Hamilton Fish, Robert C. Schenck, Samuel Nelson, Ebenezer Rockwood Hoar, and George H. Williams; on the part of Great Britain, by the Earl de Grey and Ripon, Sir Stafford H. Northcote, Sir Edward Thornton, Sir John A. Macdonald, and Mountague Bernard. This treaty provided for four distinct arbitrations, the largest number ever established under a single convention, and, by reason of this fact as well as of the magnitude of the questions submitted, was undoubtedly the greatest treaty of arbitration that the world had ever seen.

Of the four arbitrations for which it provided, the first in order and in importance was that at Geneva. On the part of the United States, the arbitrator was Charles Francis Adams; on the part of Great Britain, Sir Alexander Cockburn. There were three other arbitrators, Count Frederic Sclopis, a distinguished jurist; Jacques Staempfli, afterwards President of Switzerland; and the Viscount D'Itajuba, an eminent diplomatist, respectively designated by the King of Italy, the President of the Swiss Confederation, and the Emperor of Brazil. The American agent was J. C. Bancroft Davis; the British agent, Lord Tenderden. Caleb Cushing, William M. Evarts, and Morrison R. Waite appeared as counsel for the United States. Sir Roundell Palmer, afterwards Lord Selborne, appeared for

Great Britain, assisted by Mountague Bernard and Mr. Cohen.

The demands presented by the United States to the tribunal, arising out of the acts of Confederate cruisers of British origin, and generically known as the *Alabama* claims, embraced (1) direct losses growing out of the destructions of vessels and their cargoes by such cruisers, (2) the national expenditures in pursuit of the cruisers, (3) the loss for the transfer of the American commercial marine to the British flag, (4) the enhanced payments of insurance, and (5) the prolongation of the war and the addition of a large sum to its cost. As to classes 3, 4, and 5, Great Britain denied the jurisdiction of the tribunal; but without deciding this question, the tribunal disposed of these three classes by expressing an opinion that they did not, upon the principles of international law, constitute a good foundation for an award of compensation, and that they should be excluded from consideration, even if there were no difference between the two governments as to the board's competency. In regard to the second class of claims, the tribunal held that they were not properly distinguishable from the general expenses of the war carried on by the United States; and further, by a majority of three to two, that no compensation should be awarded to the United States on that head. On claims of the first class, the tribunal awarded the sum of $15,500,000.

Its first session was held December 15, 1871; its last, September 14, 1872.

The dispute as to the San Juan water boundary was submitted to the German Emperor, who rendered, on October 21, 1872, an award in favor of the United States. Claims of British subjects against the United States, and of citizens of the United States against Great Britain (other than the *Alabama* claims), arising out of injuries to persons or property during the civil war in the United States, from April 17, 1861, to April 9, 1865, were referred to a mixed commission, which sat in the United States. The fourth arbitration under the treaty of Washington, to determine the compensation, if any, due to Great Britain for privileges accorded by the treaty to the United States in the northeastern fisheries, was conducted by a commission of three persons—a citizen of the United States, a British subject, and a Belgian—which met at Halifax, June 15, 1877, and on the 23d of the following November awarded to Great Britain (the American commissioner dissenting) the sum of $5,500,000.

Questions of great moment, as affecting the free use of the seas, were involved in the fur-seal arbitration, which was held in Paris under the treaty of February 29, 1892; and eminent men were chosen to discuss and decide them. On the part of the United States, the arbitrators were John M. Harlan, of the Supreme Court, and John T. Morgan, of the Senate; on the part of Great Britain, Lord Hannen, of the High Court of Appeal, and Sir John Thompson, Minister of Justice and Attorney-General of Canada. The neutral arbitrators were the Baron Alphonse de Courcel, a senator and ambassador of France; the Marquis Emilio Visconti Venosta, a senator of Italy, who had held the post of Minister of Foreign Affairs; and Gregers Gram, a Minister of State of Sweden. The American agent was John W. Foster; the British agent, Sir Charles H. Tupper. As counsel for the United States, there appeared Edward J. Phelps, James C. Carter, Henry W. Blodgett, and Frederic R. Coudert; for Great Britain, Sir Charles Russell, Sir Richard Webster, and Christopher Robinson. The award which, so far as questions of jurisdiction were concerned, was unfavorable to the United States, is conceded to have been based upon existing rules of international law, the tribunal deeming its duties to be judicial rather than legislative. The commission, however, under powers expressly conferred upon it, prescribed regulations for the protection of the fur-seals by joint action. The claims of British subjects for the previous seizure of their vessels by American cruisers in Bering Sea were afterwards adjusted by a mixed commission.

The proceeding of 1903, by which the Alaskan boundary dispute was settled, can scarcely be classed as an arbitration, since the tribunal, which contained an equal number of the citizens or subjects of each contracting party, was unable to render a decision unless an appointee of one government should give his decision in favor of the other. This proved in the particular instance to be possible, Lord Alverstone (formerly Sir Richard Webster), Chief-Justice of England, one of the British members, having given the highest proof of the independence and impartiality of the British bench by joining in a decision favorable to the United States.

Down to 1898, when the controversy as to Cuba was at length settled by the sword, all differences between the United States and Spain, which could not be adjusted by diplomacy, were, beginning with the mixed commission under the Pinckney-Godoy treaty of 1795, settled by arbitration. The most important of the arbitral tribunals between the two countries was that which was established under the diplomatic agreement of February 11–12, 1871, touching claims growing out of the insurrection in Cuba. There were two other arbitrations between the two countries, held respectively in 1870 and 1880.

As between the United States and France, many important questions, including large pecuniary claims, have been settled by direct negotiation. But from November, 1880, to March, 1884, a mixed commission, sitting in Washington, disposed of the claims of citizens of France against the United States for injuries to their persons and property during the American civil war, and of the claims of citizens of the United States against France for injuries during the war between that country and Germany.

On various occasions, as under the treaties of 1839 and 1868, arbitrations have been held between the United States and Mexico. The claims submitted under the treaty of 1868 were remarkable, both in number and in amount, those presented by the United States aggregating one thousand and seventeen, and those by Mexico nine hundred and ninety-eight, while the total amount claimed on one side and the other exceeded half a billion dollars. The total amount allowed was, however, about $4,250,000. Two of the awards against Mexico, which embraced nearly or quite a third of the total amount awarded against her, were alleged to have been procured by fraudulent testimony. The government of the United States investigated this allegation, and eventually returned to Mexico all the money that had been paid by her on the awards in question, even paying out of its own treasury such part as had already been distributed among the claimants.

Arbitrations have also been held by the United States with Colombia, Costa Rica, Denmark, Ecuador, Hayti, Nicaragua, Paraguay, Peru, Portugal, Salvador, Santo Domingo, Siam, and Venezuela. The total number of the arbitrations of the United States down to 1900 was fifty-seven, twenty of which were with Great Britain, while the President of the United States had acted as arbitrator between other nations in five cases, and ministers of the United States, or persons designated by the United States, had acted as arbitrator or umpire in seven cases. The number of the arbitrations of the United States during that period was equalled only by those of Great Britain, the total of which appears to have been the same.

In adopting arbitration as a means of settling its disputes, the government of the United States has no doubt been influenced by the manifestation in various forms of public sentiment in favor of that method. As early as February, 1832, the senate of Massachusetts, by a vote of 19 to 5, resolved that "some mode should be established for the amicable and final adjustment of all international disputes instead of resort to war"; and in 1837 a like resolution was passed by the house of representatives unanimously. Similar declarations were adopted by the legislatures of other States. In 1874 a resolution in favor of general arbitration was passed by the House of Representatives of the United States.

On November 29, 1881, Mr. Blaine, as Secretary of State, extended, in the name of the President, an invitation to all the independent countries of North and South America to participate in a general congress to be held in Washington on November 24,

1882, "for the purpose of considering and discussing methods of preventing war between the nations of America." Action upon this proposal was postponed chiefly because of the continuance of the Chile-Peruvian war, but the project was never entirely relinquished, and on May 28, 1888, the President gave his approval to the act under which was convoked the International American Conference of 1889–1890. Of this conference one of the results was the celebrated plan of arbitration adopted April 18, 1890. By this plan it was declared that arbitration, as a means of settling disputes between American republics, was adopted "as a principle of American international law"; that arbitration should be obligatory in all controversies concerning diplomatic and consular privileges, boundaries, territories, indemnities, the right of navigation, and the validity, construction, and enforcement of treaties; and that it should be equally obligatory in all other cases, whatever might be their origin, nature, or object, with the sole exception of those which, in the judgment of one of the nations involved in the controversy, might imperil its independence; but that, even in this case, while arbitration for that nation should be optional, it should be "obligatory upon the adversary power." As yet this plan represents but an aspiration, since it failed to receive the approval of the governments whose representatives adopted it.

On February 14, 1890, the Senate of the United States, and on the 3d of the following April the House of Representatives, adopted a concurrent resolution by which the President was requested to invite, from time to time as fit occasions might arise, negotiations with any government with which the United States maintained diplomatic relations, "to the end that any differences or disputes arising between the two governments which cannot be adjusted by diplomatic agency may be referred to arbitration, and be peaceably adjusted by such means." On July 16, 1893, the British House of Commons formally declared its cordial sympathy with the purpose of this resolution, and expressed the hope that her Majesty's government would "lend their ready co-operation to the government of the United States" upon the basis indicated.

Nothing tangible had been accomplished in that direction when the controversy over the Venezuelan boundary disclosed the importance of arbitration as a possible means of avoiding a conflict between the two countries. Under these circumstances, Mr. Olney, as Secretary of State, negotiated with Sir Julian Pauncefote, then British ambassador at Washington, concurrently with the negotiation of a special treaty of arbitration for the settlement of the Venezuelan question, a general arbitration treaty. By this treaty, provision was made for three classes of tribunals, two of which were to be boards of three or five members, as the case might be, while the third was to be, not in strictness a tribunal of arbitration, but a joint commission, in the form lately employed in the Alaskan boundary dispute, specifically to deal with territorial claims. This treaty failed to receive the approval of the necessary two-thirds of the Senate, but only by a few votes.

In the peace conference that met at The Hague, in 1899, on the invitation of the Czar of Russia, the United States was one of the participants. Of this conference, the most notable achievement was the convention for the peaceful adjustment of international differences. This convention embraces stipulations, first, as to mediation, and secondly, as to arbitration. In the part relating to mediation, the signatory powers agree that, in case of "grave difference of opinion or conflict," they will, before appealing to arms, have recourse, "as far as circumstances permit," to the good offices of one or more friendly powers, and that such powers even may of their own motion offer mediation, without incurring the odium of performing an unfriendly act. The functions of the mediator are, however, declared to be purely conciliatory, and his recommendations "advisory" and not "obligatory." As an adjunct to the system of mediation the convention recommends in certain cases the appointment of an international commission of inquiry, the mode of whose appointment, as well as its jurisdiction and procedure, is to be regulated by a special convention between the disputing states.

By the arbitral stipulations, the object of international arbitration is declared to be "the settlement of disputes between nations by judges of their own choice and in accordance with their reciprocal rights"; and arbitration is recognized as specially applicable to questions of law, and of the interpretation and execution of treaties, which cannot be settled by diplomacy. The resort to arbitration is voluntary, but the convention furnishes a plan by which it is intended to be systematized and made easy. Of this plan the basal feature is what is called the permanent court of arbitration, which is constituted by the designation by each of the signatory powers of not more than four persons "recognized as competent to deal with questions of international law, and of the highest personal integrity." The persons so designated, who are known as "members of the court," constitute a list from which any of the signatory powers, in the event of a controversy, may, if they see fit to do so, choose a tribunal for the decision of the particular case.

To the existence of this convention there is, no doubt, to be ascribed the recent remarkable agreement between Great Britain and Russia for the settlement, by means of a mixed court of inquiry, of the Dogger Bank incident.

The subject of general arbitration between American nations, which remained in abeyance after the Washington conference of 1890, was again taken up by the Second International Conference of American States, which met at the city of Mexico on October 22, 1901. There appeared to be, as the American members of the conference reported, a unanimous sentiment in favor of "arbitration as a principle," but a great contrariety of opinion as to the extent to which the principle should be carried. A plan was finally adopted in the nature of a compromise. A protocol looking to adhesion to The Hague convention was signed by all the delegations except those of Chile and Ecuador, who are said, however, afterwards to have accepted it in open conference. A project of a treaty of compulsory arbitration was also signed by the delegations of certain countries, not including the United States, and a treaty was also adopted covering the arbitration of pecuniary claims.

When we consider the future of international arbitration, whether in America or elsewhere, we are at once confronted with the question as to its limitations. Is it possible to fix any precise bounds, beyond which this mode of settling international disputes may be said to be impracticable? If we consult the history of arbitrations during the past hundred years, we are obliged to answer that no such lines can be definitely drawn; but this is far from affirming that the use of force in the conduct of international affairs will soon be abolished. It signifies merely that phrases such as "national honor" and "national self-defence," which have been employed in describing supposed exceptions to the principle of arbitration, convey no definitive meaning. Questions of honor and of self-defence are, in international as in private relations, matters partly of circumstance and partly of opinion. When the United States, in 1863, first proposed that the differences that had arisen with Great Britain, as to the fitting out of the *Alabama* and other Confederate cruisers, should be submitted to arbitration, Earl Russell rejected the overture on the ground that the questions in controversy involved the honor of her Majesty's government, of which that government was declared to be "the sole guardian." Eight years later there was concluded at Washington the treaty under which the differences between the two governments were submitted to the judgment of the tribunal that met at Geneva. This remarkable example serves to illustrate the fact that the scope and progress of arbitration will depend, not so much upon special devices, or upon general declarations or descriptive exceptions, as upon the dispositions of nations, dispositions which, although they are subject to the modifying influence of public opinion, spring primarily from the national feelings, the national interests, and the national ambitions.

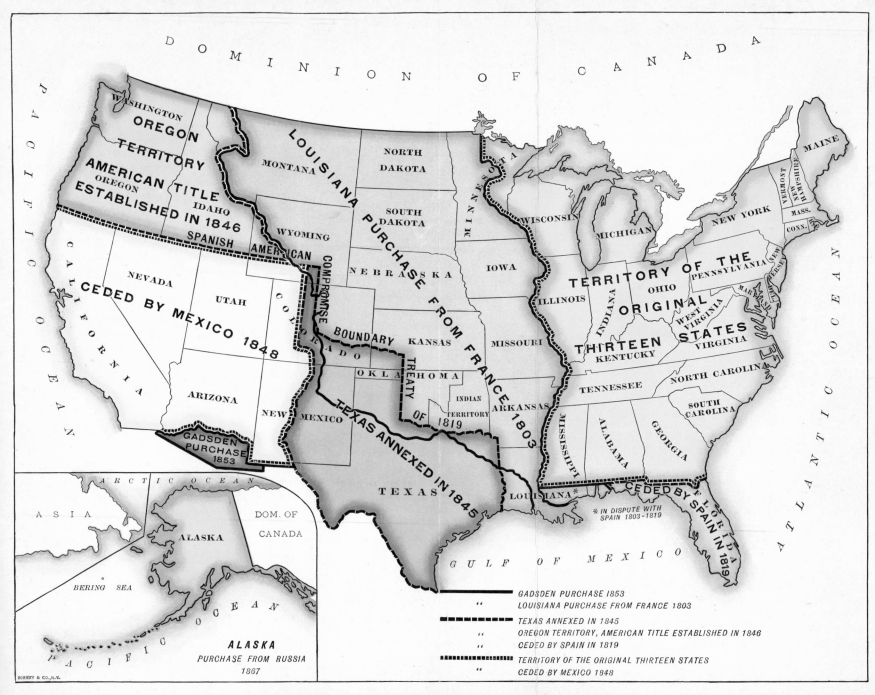

CONTINENTAL EXPANSION OF THE UNITED STATES

IX

THE TERRITORIAL EXPANSION OF THE UNITED STATES

As conventionalized in the annual messages of Presidents to Congress, the American people are distinguished chiefly by their peaceful disposition and their freedom from territorial ambitions. Nevertheless, in spite of these quiet propensities, it has fallen to their lot, since they forcibly achieved their independence, to have had four foreign wars, three general and one limited, and the greatest civil war in history, and to have acquired a territorial domain almost five times as great as the respectable endowment with which they began their national career. In reality, to the founders of the American Republic the question of territorial expansion did not present itself as a matter of speculation, or even of choice. There was not a single European power having possessions in America that did not lay claim to more territory than it had effectively occupied, nor was there a single one whose claims were not contested by some other power; and these contests were interwoven with the monopolistic struggle then in progress for colonial commerce and navigation. The Spaniards and the Portuguese, the English and the French, the Swedes and the Dutch, contended with one another in Europe as well as in America for empire on the American continents. Their colonists knew no rule of life but that of conflict; and they regarded the extension of their boundaries as a measure of self-defence rather than of aggression. We have seen that, by the treaty of alliance with France of 1778, the remaining British possession in North America, if they should be wrested from the mother-country, were to be "confederated with or dependent upon" the United States; and in harmony with this stipulation, provision was made in the Articles of Confederation (Article xi.) for the full admission of Canada into the Union. No other colony was to be so admitted without the consent of nine States; and unless they consented, the colony, if seized, was to remain in a "dependent" position. With the independence of the United States, a new force entered into the territorial contests in America, but it did not stay their course. On the north of the new republic lay the possessions of Great Britain; on the west, the possessions of France; on the south, the possessions of Spain. With all these powers there were questions of boundary, while the colonial restrictions in commerce and in navigation were as so many withes by which the limbs of the young giant were fettered.

It was in order to obtain relief from such condi-

tions that the United States acquired Louisiana.
To the inhabitants of the West, the Mississippi
River was, as Madison once declared, the Hudson,
the Delaware, the Potomac, and all the navigable
rivers of the Atlantic States formed into one stream.
During the dark hours of the American Revolution,
the Continental Congress seemed to be ready to
yield to Spain, in return for her alliance, the exclusive right to navigate the Mississippi; but for-
tunately this was not done. After the re-establishment of peace, Spain continued to maintain her
exclusive claims. But the opposition to them in
the United States steadily grew stronger and louder;
and at length, on October 27, 1795, encompassed
by many perils in her foreign relations, Spain conceded to the United States the free navigation of the
Mississippi, together with the privilege of depositing
merchandise at New Orleans and thence exporting
it without payment of duty. The incalculable advantage of this arrangement was daily growing more
manifest when, early in 1801, rumors began to prevail that Spain had ceded both Louisiana and the
Floridas to France. As a neighbor, Spain, because
of the internal weakness of her government and the
consequent unaggressiveness of her foreign policy,
was not feared; but an apprehension had from the
first been exhibited by the United States as to the
possibility of being hemmed in by colonies of England and France. If the rumored cession should

15

prove to be true, the arrangement with Spain with regard to the Mississippi was threatened with extinction. Jefferson was therefore hardly extravagant when he declared that the cession of Louisiana and the Floridas by Spain to France would completely reverse all the political relations of the United States, and would render France, as the possessor of New Orleans, "our natural and habitual enemy."

The treaty of cession was in fact signed at San Ildefonso, on October 1, 1800; but it was not published and even its existence was officially denied. It did not embrace the Floridas, but included the whole of the vast domain then known as Louisiana. The administration at Washington, though in the dark as to what had actually been done, felt the necessity of action. It desired if possible to prevent the transfer of the territory; or, if this could not be accomplished, to obtain from France the Floridas, if they were included in the cession, or at least West Florida, so as to give the United States a continuous stretch of territory on the eastern bank of the Mississippi. With these objects in view, Jefferson appointed Robert R. Livingston as minister to France. Livingston set out on his mission early in October, 1801. On his arrival in Paris he soon became convinced that the cession of Louisiana, if not of the Floridas, had been concluded; and he hinted to Talleyrand, who was then Minister of

Foreign Affairs, that Louisiana might be transferred to the United States in payment of debts due by France to American citizens. Talleyrand replied, "None but spendthrifts satisfy their debts by selling their lands," and then, after a pause, blandly added, "But it is not ours to give." Livingston was not deceived by this evasion; on the contrary, he endeavored to obtain, by appeal to the First Consul himself, Napoleon, the cession, not of the whole but of a part of Louisiana, or at any rate an assurance that the transfer of the territory by Spain to France would not be permitted to disturb the arrangement as to the use of the Mississippi. On February 11, 1802, Talleyrand informed Livingston that he had been instructed by the First Consul to give the most positive assurance on this subject; but it had barely been given, when a report reached Washington that the Spanish intendant at New Orleans had suspended the right of deposit. It was soon learned that the suspension was not authorized by the Spanish government, but the act of the intendant gave rise to energetic discussions in Congress. A resolution was adopted by the House declaring that the stipulated rights of the United States in the Mississippi would be inviolably maintained, while a resolution was offered in the Senate to authorize the President to take forcible possession of such places as might be necessary to secure their full enjoyment. The state of public feeling was such that every branch of the government felt obliged to take measures not only to preserve existing rights, but also, if possible, to enlarge and safeguard them. With this end in view, James Monroe was joined with Livingston in an extraordinary commission to treat with France, and with Charles Pinckney in a like commission to treat, if necessary, with Spain. The specific objects of the mission, as defined in the instructions given by Madison, as Secretary of State, on March 2, 1803, were the cession to the United States of the island of New Orleans and the Floridas.

Meanwhile, Livingston had, if possible, redoubled his exertions. His favorite plan was to obtain from France the cession of the island of New Orleans and all that part of Louisiana lying northward of the Arkansas River; and he also urged the cession of West Florida, if France had obtained it from Spain. On Monday, April 11th, he held with Talleyrand a memorable and startling interview. Livingston was expatiating upon the subject of New Orleans, when Talleyrand quietly inquired whether the United States desired the "whole of Louisiana." Livingston answered that their wishes extended only to New Orleans and the Floridas, though policy dictated that France should also cede the country above the river Arkansas; but Talleyrand observed that, if they gave New Orleans, the rest would be of little value, and asked what the United States would "give for the whole." Livingston suggested the sum of 20,000,000 francs, provided the claims of American citizens were paid. Talleyrand declared the offer too low, but disclaimed having spoken of the matter by authority. In reality Napoleon had, on the preceding day, announced to two of his ministers his final resolution. The expedition to Santo Domingo had miserably failed; colonial enterprises appeared to be no longer practicable; war with England was at hand; and it seemed wiser to sell colonies than go down with them in disaster. In this predicament Napoleon decided to sell to the United States not only New Orleans but the whole of Louisiana, and only a few hours before the interview between Talleyrand and Livingston was held, had instructed Barbé Marbois, his Minister of Finance, to negotiate the sale.

Monroe arrived in Paris on April 12th. On the next day Marbois informed Livingston that Napoleon had authorized him to say that, if the Americans would give 100,000,000 francs and pay their own claims, they might "take the whole country." Noting Livingston's surprise at the price, Marbois eventually suggested that the United States should pay to France the sum of 60,000,000 francs and assume the claims of its own citizens to the amount of 20,000,000 more. Livingston declared that it was in vain to ask a thing so greatly beyond their means, but promised to consult with Monroe. The American plenipotentiaries were thus confronted with a momentous question concerning which in its full extent their instructions did not authorize them to treat; but properly interpreting the purposes of their government and the spirit of their countrymen, they promptly and boldly assumed the responsibility. They accepted Marbois's terms, excessive as they at first seemed, and took the whole province. Speaking in a prophetic strain, Livingston, when he had affixed his name to the treaty of cession, exclaimed: "We have lived long, but this is the noblest work of our lives. . . . To-day the United States take their place among the powers of the first rank. . . . The instrument we have signed will cause no tears to flow. It will prepare centuries of happiness for innumerable generations of the human race." Time has verified Livingston's prevision. The purchase of Louisiana has contributed more than any other territorial acquisition to make the United States what it is to-day.

Though the whole of Louisiana was ceded, its limits were undefined. The province was retroceded by Spain to France in 1800 "with the same extent that it now has in the hands of Spain, and that it had when France possessed it," and by the treaty of April 30, 1803, the territory was ceded to the United States "in the same manner," but the boundaries had never been precisely determined. Livingston and Monroe assured their government that the cession extended to the river Perdido, and

ROBERT R. LIVINGSTON

therefore embraced West Florida. This claim was not sanctioned by France, but Congress, acting upon Livingston and Monroe's assurance, authorized the President in his discretion to erect "the bay and river Mobile" and the adjacent territory into a customs district. Spain strongly protested, and the execution of the measure was held in suspense. In the summer of 1810, however, a revolution took place in West Florida. Baton Rouge was seized; the independence of the province was declared; and an application was made for its admission into the Union. The President repulsed this application, but occupied the territory, as far as the river Pearl, as part of the Louisiana purchase. The country lying between that stream and the Perdido was permitted still to remain in the possession of Spain.

On January 3, 1811, President Madison, incited by the political situation in America as well as in Europe, sent to Congress a secret message, in which he recommended that the Executive be authorized to take temporary possession of any part of the Floridas, in certain contingencies. As to West Florida, Congress had already clothed the Executive with ample powers; but as East Florida unquestionably still belonged to Spain, Congress authorized the President to occupy all or any part of the country, either under arrangements with the local authorities or in case a foreign government should attempt to seize it. Under this act, East Florida was taken possession of all the way from Fernandina to St. Augustine; but the manner in which it was done was disapproved by the government at Washington, and in May, 1813, the country was finally evacuated by the American forces. During the war of 1812, West Florida was the scene of hostilities between the British and the American forces, and in 1817 and 1818 it was the theatre of the famous Seminole war. Meanwhile the government of the United States was endeavoring to obtain from Spain the relinquishment of her provinces. The negotiations, which were conducted on the part of the United States by John Quincy Adams, were brought to a close by the treaty of February 22, 1819, by which Spain ceded to the United States not only the Floridas, but also all the Spanish titles north of the forty-second parallel of north latitude from the source of the Arkansas River to the Pacific Ocean. In return, the United States agreed to pay the claims of its citizens against Spain to an amount not exceeding $5,000,-000, and to indemnify the Spanish inhabitants of the Floridas for injuries suffered at the hands of American forces, besides granting to Spanish commerce in the ceded territories, for the term of twelve years, exceptional privileges.

While the United States retained under the treaty of 1819 all the territory to the eastward that it claimed as part of Louisiana, it relinquished by the

same treaty its claim to the imperial domain called
Texas, a province long in dispute between France
and Spain, and after 1803 between Spain and the
United States. Only a brief time, however, elapsed
when efforts began to be made to recover Texas,
either in whole or in part. Two such attempts were
made during the Presidency of John Quincy Adams,
in 1825 and 1827. The effort was renewed by President Jackson in 1829, and again in 1833. In August,
1835, the American minister in Mexico was directed
to persevere in the task, and also to offer half a
million dollars for the bay of San Francisco and certain adjacent territory as a resort for American
vessels in the Pacific. On March 2, 1836, the people of Texas, through a convention of delegates, declared their independence. In the following year
President Van Buren repelled an overture for annexation. The independence of Texas was, however, acknowledged not only by the United States,
but also by France and Great Britain; and treaties
were made with Texas by all those powers. On
April 12, 1844, a treaty of annexation was concluded
at Washington. This treaty having failed in the
Senate, Congress, by a joint resolution approved
March 1, 1845, took action looking to the admission
of Texas into the Union as a State. The terms offered in the resolution were accepted by Texas, and
by a joint resolution of Congress, approved December 29, 1845, the admission was formally accom-

plished. No acquisition of territory by the United States has been the subject of so much honest but partisan misconception as that of the annexation of Texas. By a school of writers whose views have had great currency, the annexation has been denounced as the result of a plot of the slave-power to extend its dominions. But, calmly surveying the course of American expansion, we are forced to conclude that no illusion could be more complete. It would be more nearly correct to say that, but for the controversy concerning slavery, there would have been no appreciable opposition in the United States to the acquisition of Texas. Such local antagonism as might have existed to the disturbance of the balance of power in the Union would have been overwhelmed by the general demand for an extension of boundaries so natural and, except for the slavery question, in every respect so expedient.

Six months after the annexation of Texas, the long dispute as to the Oregon territory was brought to a close. This territory was bounded, according to the claim of the United States, by the 42d parallel of north latitude on the south, by the line of 54° 40′ on the north, and by the Rocky or Stony Mountains on the east. It embraced, roughly speaking, an area of 600,000 square miles. The claim of the United States was founded upon the discovery by Captain Robert Gray, of the American ship *Columbia*, in 1792, of the River of the West, which he named from his ship the Columbia River; the exploration of the main branch of that river by Lewis and Clark; the establishment of the fur-trading settlement of Astoria, by John Jacob Astor, in 1811, and its restoration to the United States under the treaty of Ghent; and finally, the acquisition in 1819 of all the territorial rights of Spain on the Pacific above forty-second degree of north latitude. By the Democratic national platform of 1844 the title of the United States to the whole of Oregon was declared to be "clear and unquestionable." This declaration was popularly interpreted to mean "fifty-four forty or fight"; but on June 15, 1846, under the shadow of the Mexican war, the dispute was terminated by a nearly equal division of the territory along the forty-ninth parallel of north latitude.

This title had barely been assured, when, as the result of the war with Mexico, the United States, by the treaty signed on its behalf by Nicholas P. Trist, in defiance of instructions, at Guadalupe-Hidalgo, on February 2, 1848, came into possession of California and New Mexico. In consideration of these cessions, the United States paid to Mexico $15,000,000, and assumed the payment of claims of American citizens against Mexico to an amount not exceeding $3,250,000. The acquisitions thus made were enlarged by the convention of December 30, 1853, by which Mexico, for the sum of $10,000,-000, released the United States from liability on account of certain stipulations of the treaty of 1848 and ceded the Mesilla Valley. This cession, which is often called the Gadsden purchase, was strongly desired by the United States, not only for the purpose of establishing a safe frontier against the Indians, but also for the purpose of obtaining a feasible route for a railway near the Gila River.

By the treaty signed at Washington on March 30, 1867, the Emperor of Russia, in consideration of the sum of $7,200,000, conveyed to the United States all his "territory and dominion" in America. Many strange conjectures have been made as to the motives of this transaction. It has been suggested that it was merely a cover for the reimbursement to Russia of the expenses of her "friendly naval demonstration" during the American civil war. This explanation may be placed in the category of the grotesque. Robert J. Walker has been given as authority for the statement that the Emperor Nicholas was ready to give Alaska to the United States during the Crimean war, if the United States would, in spite of the treaty of 1846, reassert its claim to the whole of Oregon. In reality, the territory was of comparatively small value to Russia, who had for years leased an important part of the coast to the Hudson's Bay Company. In the hands of the United States its potential value was obviously greater. Its acquisition was, besides, gratifying to the spirit of continental dominion, which has always been so strongly manifested by the people of the United States.

The acquisition of the Hawaiian Islands, under the joint resolution of Congress of July 7, 1898, marked the natural consummation of the special relations that had long subsisted between the United States and that island group. As early as 1853 the United States, while William L. Marcy was Secretary of State, sought to annex the islands. A treaty of annexation was negotiated, but, as its form was unacceptable to the United States, it was put aside for a treaty of reciprocity. This treaty failed to receive the approval of the Senate, but the agitation for annexation or reciprocity continued; and at length, on January 30, 1875, a reciprocity treaty was concluded by which the islands were virtually placed under an American protectorate. This treaty was renewed in 1887, the United States then acquiring the right to establish a naval station in the harbor of Pearl River. On February 14, 1893, a treaty of annexation was signed at Washington, but on the change of administration it was withdrawn from the Senate. Another treaty of annexation, signed on June 16, 1897, was still before the Senate when the joint resolution was passed by which the acquisition was definitively accomplished.

Alaska and Hawaii were far distant from the United States, but the greater part of Alaska was on the continent of North America, and the Hawaiian Islands had so long been the subject of special protection as to have come to be considered within the sphere of American influence. The war with Spain opened a new vista. Even the remotest of the Spanish possessions in the West Indies fell within the conception of America, but the Spanish possessions in the Far East lay beyond the accustomed range of American political thought. For some weeks after the destruction of the Spanish fleet at Manila, the views of the United States seemed scarcely to extend beyond the possible acquisition of a naval station in the Philippines for strategic purposes. The desire for a naval station, however, soon grew into the desire for an island—perhaps the island of Luzon. When news came of the capture of Manila by the American forces, with some American casualties, the desire for the whole group received a marked impulse. In his instructions to the American peace commissioners at Paris, President McKinley said that the United States would not be content with "less than" the island of Luzon. More than two months elapsed before instructions were given to take the whole group; and even then, as the records show, the American commissioners were divided on the question. For my own part, I venture to express the opinion that the problem was simplified by taking all the islands. Though the group is vast in extent, it is physically continuous, and, if a considerable part of it had been retained by Spain, the dangers attendant upon native revolt and discontent would have been incalculably increased. The acquisition of Puerto Rico and other Spanish islands in the West Indies provoked no division of opinion.

There is no incident in the history of the United States that better prepares us to understand the acquisition of the Philippines than the course of the government towards the Samoan Islands. As early as 1853, if not earlier, the United States was represented at Apia by a commercial agent; but the islands and their affairs attracted little attention till 1872, when the great chief of the bay of Pago-Pago (pronounced Pango-Pango), in the island of Tutuila, desirous of obtaining the protection of the United States, granted to the government the exclusive privilege of establishing a naval station in that harbor. A special agent, named Steinberger, was then despatched to Samoa, and, after making a report, he was sent back to convey to the chiefs a letter from President Grant and some presents. Subsequently he set up, on his own responsibility, a government in the islands and administered it. But as ruler of Samoa he fell into difficulties, and, with the concurrence of the American consul, was deported on a British man-of-war. On January 16, 1878, a treaty between the United States and Samoa was concluded at Washington, by which the privileges of the United States in the harbor of Pago-Pago were confirmed, and by which it was provided that, if differences shall arise between the Samoan government and any other government in amity with the United States, the latter would "employ its good offices for the purpose of adjusting those differences upon a satisfactory and solid foundation." It was under this clause that the conference, which was held in Washington in June and July, 1887, between Mr. Bayard, as Secretary of State, and the British and German ministers, on Samoan affairs, was brought about. The conference failed to produce an agreement. Germany intervened in the islands, and became involved in hostilities with a part of the natives. Steps were taken to protect American interests, and the relations between the United States and Germany had become decidedly strained when, on the invitation of Prince Bismarck, the sessions of the conference were resumed at Berlin. They resulted in the treaty of June 14, 1889, by which the islands were placed under the joint protection and administration of the three powers. The cumbersome system of tripartite government thus established signally failed; and at length, by a treaty between the three powers, concluded on December 2, 1899, Tutuila and the adjacent islands, east of longitude 171° west of Greenwich, passed under the jurisdiction of the United States, while Upolu and Savaii, and other islands west of that meridian, were left to Germany. The significance of the Samoan incident lies, however, not in the mere division of territory, but in the disposition shown by the United States, long before the acquisition of the Philippines, to have a voice in determining the fate of a remote island group in which American commercial interests were so slight as to be scarcely appreciable.

By the convention with the Republic of Panama, November 18, 1903, the United States acquired in perpetuity the use, occupation, and control of a zone ten miles wide on the Isthmus of Panama, and certain adjacent islands, for the purposes of an interoceanic canal. Within these lands and the adjacent waters the United States possesses "all the rights, power, and authority" which it would have if it were the sovereign of the territory within which the lands and waters lie. It may be observed that an unsuccessful effort was made in 1856 to obtain from New Granada the cession of five islands in the bay of Panama, with a view to protect the isthmian route.

Besides the annexations already described, the United States has acquired or assumed jurisdiction over many islands in various parts of the world. In 1850, the cession was obtained from Great Britain of Horse-Shoe Reef, in Lake Erie, for the purposes of a light-house. In 1867, Brooks or Midway Islands, lying 1100 miles west of Honolulu, were formally occupied by the commander of the U. S. S. *Lackawanna*. In like manner the atoll called Wake Island, lying in latitude 19° 17′ 50″ north and longitude 166° 31′ east, was taken possession of in 1899 by the commander of the U. S. S. *Bennington*. But the greatest extension of jurisdiction over detached islands or groups of islands has taken place under the Guano Islands Act of August 18, 1856. By this act, where an American citizen discovers a deposit of guano on an island, rock, or key, not within the jurisdiction of any other government, and takes peaceable possession and gives a certain bond, the President may, at his discretion, treat the territory as "appertaining to the United States"; but the government is not obliged to retain possession after the guano shall have been removed. Under this statute more than eighty islands, lying in various parts of the Atlantic and the Pacific, have been brought within American jurisdiction.

The actual acquisitions of territory by the United States by no means indicate the scope of its diplomatic activities in that direction. Efforts have been made to annex territory which has not eventually been obtained. As late as 1870 the annexation of Canada, to which the Articles of Confederation looked, was the subject of informal discussions between British and American diplomatists. In December, 1822, the government of Salvador, acting under a decree of its Congress, despatched three commissioners to Washington to offer the sovereignty of the country to the United States, but before their arrival the situation had changed and the proposal was abandoned. Ever since the foundation of the American Republic, the annexation of Cuba has formed a topic of discussion and of diplomatic activity. John Quincy Adams in 1823 declared that Cuba, if forcibly disjoined from Spain, and incapable of self-support, could gravitate only towards the North American Union; and Jefferson confessed that he had "ever looked on Cuba as the most interesting addition which could ever be made to our system of States." In 1848 an offer was made to Spain to purchase the island for $100,000,-000, but it was summarily repulsed. During the civil war in the United States, the discussion of the Cuban question, which had actively continued during the administrations of Pierce and Buchanan, was suspended; but it was revived by the breaking out of the Ten Years' War in Cuba, in 1868. In the next year a vigorous effort was made to secure the separation of Cuba from Spain either by annexation to the United States or by the grant of independence under the guarantee of the United States. This was the last definite proposal made to Spain for annexation, and, when the United States eventually intervened, it was for the purpose of establishing Cuban independence. In the peace negotiations at Paris, the Spanish commissioners proposed to cede the island to the United States. The proposal was declined; and the manner in which the resolution of intervention was kept, by the establishment of an independent government under safeguards which cannot hamper the exercise of the island's sovereignty for any legitimate purpose, forms one of the most honorable chapters in diplomatic history.

In 1848 an offer of the sovereignty of Yucatan was made to the United States, but the occasion for its consideration soon passed away.

In negotiations with the Dominican Republic, in 1854, for a commercial treaty, an effort was made to obtain for the United States a coaling station in Samana Bay. An examination of the bay had been made by Captain George B. McClellan, whose report may be found among the Congressional documents. The effort to obtain the desired privilege was renewed in 1855, but without success. In 1866, Mr. F. W. Seward, Assistant Secretary of State, was sent to Santo Domingo for the purpose of securing a cession or lease of the peninsula of Samana as a naval station. His mission was not successful, but its object was not abandoned, and his powers were transferred to the commercial agent at Santo Domingo City. In 1868 the President of the Dominican Republic requested the United States immediately to take the country under its protection and occupy Samana Bay and other strategic points as a preliminary to annexation. In his annual message of December 9, 1868, President Johnson, Mr. Seward still being Secretary of State, advocated the acquisition of "the several adjacent continental and insular communities as speedily as it may be done peacefully, lawfully, and without any violation of national justice, faith, or honor," and declared that, while foreign possession or control of them had "hindered the growth and impaired the influence of the United States," "chronic revolution and anarchy would be equally injurious." A joint resolution was introduced in the House of Representatives for the annexation of the Dominican Republic. An agent from Santo Domingo was then in Washington awaiting action. The project was warmly espoused by President Grant, and on November 29, 1869, two treaties were concluded, one for the annexation of the Dominican Republic and the other for the lease of Samana Bay. Both instruments were communicated to the Senate on January 10, 1870. They failed to receive that body's approval. In his last annual message to Congress, in 1876, President Grant recurred to the subject, reaffirming his belief in the wisdom of the policy that he had proposed.

In 1867, George Bancroft was instructed, while proceeding as minister to Berlin, to call at Madrid and sound the Spanish government as to the cession of the islands of Culebra and Culebrita, in the Spanish West Indies, to the United States as a naval station. The results of his inquiries were so discouraging that the subject was peremptorily dropped; but the islands have come into the possession of the United States under the treaty of peace with Spain of 1898.

In his efforts to obtain the cession of islands in the West Indies, Mr. Seward did not overlook the Danish possessions in that quarter. His informal negotiations probably began as early as January, 1865. The Danish government discouraged his advances, but they were renewed in an official form in July, 1866. A convention for the cession of St. Thomas and St. John for $7,500,000, leaving Santa Cruz to Denmark, was signed at Copenhagen on October 24, 1867. As stipulated in the treaty, a vote was taken in the islands; it was almost unanimously in favor of annexation to the United States. This circumstance greatly increased the embarrassment of the Danish government when the United States Senate failed to approve the treaty. On January 24, 1902, a convention was signed at Washington for the cession to the United States of the islands of St. Thomas, St. John, and Santa Cruz, with the adjacent islands and rocks, all for the sum of $5,000,000. It was approved by the Senate on February 17, 1902. It was approved by the lower house of the Danish Rigsdag; but on October 21, 1902, it failed in the upper house, by an even division.

The Mole St. Nicolas, in Hayti, was leased by the United States during the civil war as a naval station. In 1891, however, the Haytian government declined to let the harbor again for a similar purpose.

X

INFLUENCE AND TENDENCIES

NOTHING could have been further from the thoughts of the wise statesmen who guided the United States through the struggle for independence and laid the foundations of the government's foreign policy than the institution of a philosophical propagandism for the dissemination of political principles of a certain type in foreign lands. Although the Declaration of Independence loudly proclaimed the theory of the natural rights of man, they gave to this theory, in its application to their own concerns, a qualified interpretation, and, as practical men, forbore to push it at once to all its logical consequences. On the continent of Europe, the apostles of reform, directing their shafts against absolutism and class privileges, spoke in terms of philosophical idealism, while the patriots of America, though they did not eschew philosophy, debated concrete questions of constitutional law and commonplace problems of taxation. In Europe, the revolution meant first of all a destructive upheaval; in America, where the ground was clear, it meant a constructive development. And yet, in spite of this difference, the American Revolution operated as a powerful stimulus to political agitation in Europe. There was in the very existence of American independence, permeated as it was with democratic republicanism, a force that exerted a world-wide influence in behalf of political liberty. Of this fact European statesmen betrayed their appreciation when they deprecated the course of the King of France in subordinating what appeared to them to be a permanent general interest to the gratification of a feeling of enmity towards Great Britain. Spanish diplomatists were not alone in expressing this sentiment. The Emperor Joseph II. of Austria, in a letter to his minister in the Netherlands, in 1787, remarked that "France, by the assistance which she afforded to the Americans, gave birth to reflections on freedom." That the assistance thus given hastened her own revolution, there can be no doubt. Nor did the visible effect of the example of the United States end here. It has been manifest in every European struggle for more liberal forms of government during the past hundred years — in Spain, in Italy, in Germany, and in Hungary. It penetrated even to Russia, where there was found among the papers of one of the leaders who planned a revolution for 1826 a constitution for that country on the model of the Constitution of the United States. And it may also be traced in the lives of those who have striven to advance, sometimes under adverse and discouraging conditions, the cause of self-government on the American continents.

While the United States refrained from aggressive political propagandism, the spirit of liberty that resulted from its independence was necessarily reflected in its diplomacy. It is true that the attitude of the government on certain special questions was for a long while affected by the survival in the United States of the institution of African slavery. It was for this reason that the recognition of Hayti, Santo Domingo, and Liberia as independent states did not take place till the administration of Abraham Lincoln, although such recognition had long before been accorded by European powers. But the attitude of the United States towards those countries was exceptional, and was governed by forces which neither diverted nor sought to divert the government from the general support of the principles on which it was founded.

The influence of the United States in behalf of political liberty was clearly exhibited in the establishment of the principle, to which we have heretofore adverted, that the true test of a government's right to exist, and to be recognized by other governments, is the fact of its existence as the exponent of the popular will. This rule, when it was announced, appeared to be little short of revolutionary, since it was in effect a corollary of the affirmation made in the Declaration of Independence, that governments derive their just powers from the consent of the governed, and that, whenever any form of government becomes destructive of the ends for which governments are instituted, it is the right of the people to alter or abolish it and to institute a new government, laying its foundation on such principles and organizing its affairs in such form as to them shall seem most likely to effect their safety and happiness. Nor was the free spirit of American diplomacy less manifest in its opposition to the system of commercial monopoly; in its espousal of the principles of the Monroe Doctrine; or in its advocacy of the freedom of the seas, of the rule that free ships make free goods, and of the exemption of private property at sea from capture. The weight of its influence was also constantly lent in favor of the maintenance of the independence of the countries of the Far East. In the treaty with China of June 18, 1858, made at a time when the Chinese government appeared to be peculiarly friendless, we find the remarkable stipulation that "if any other nation should act unjustly or oppressively" towards that country, the United States would "exert its good offices, on being informed of the case, to bring about an amicable arrangement of the question, thus showing their friendly feelings."

But, besides exerting an influence in favor of liberty and independence, American diplomacy was also employed in the advancement of the principle of legality.

American statesmen sought to regulate the relations of nations by law, not only as a measure for the protection of the weak against the aggressions of the strong, but also as the only means of assuring the peace of the world. The conception of legality in international relations lay at the foundation of the system of neutrality, which was established during the administration of Washington. It also formed the basis of the practice of arbitration, which was so auspiciously begun at the same time. Half a century later it received an accession of strength in the development of the process of extradition. It is true that in the development of this process in modern times the credit of the initiative belongs to France; but, beginning with the Webster-Ashburton treaty of August 9, 1842, the United States, at an important stage in the history of the system, actively contributed to its growth by the conclusion of numerous conventions. The twenty-seventh article of the Jay treaty provided for the surrender of fugitives charged with murder or forgery; but it proved to be for the most part ineffective, and expired by limitation in 1808. The Webster-Ashburton treaty provided for the extradition of fugitives for any of seven offences, and proved to be efficacious. Similar treaties with other countries were soon afterwards made, ten being concluded while William L. Marcy was Secretary of State, during the administration of Pierce. Since that time our extradition arrangements have grown both in number and in comprehensiveness. We cannot afford, however, to rest on our laurels. In recent times other nations, and especially Great Britain since 1870, observing the propensity of criminals to utilize improved facilities of travel, have by legislation as well as by negotiation vastly increased the reach and efficiency of the system. It will therefore be necessary, if we would fulfil the promise of our past and retain a place in the front rank, steadily to multiply our treaties and enlarge their scope. No innovation in the practice of nations has ever more completely discredited the woful predictions of its adversaries than that of surrendering fugitives from justice. The Webster-Ashburton treaty was loudly denounced as a mere trap for the recovery of political offenders. Other treaties encountered similar opposition. In no instance have these direful forebodings been justified by the event.

American diplomacy has also been characterized by practicality. It has sought to attain definite objects by practical methods. Even in its idealism, as in the advocacy of the exemption of private property at sea from capture, it has shown a practical side. The same disposition has been exhibited in the American consular service. Consuls have been described by publicists as agents of commerce; but for a long while their functions were passive rather than active, and to some extent were ornamental. The government of the United States conceived the idea of employing its consuls not only for the protection of commerce, but also for its extension. In 1880, while Mr. Evarts was Secretary of State, there was begun the monthly publication of consular reports, which has been continued with useful results up to the present time. The example thus set has been followed in other countries, so that we find to-day among the publications of the British, French, and German governments consular reports on the commerce and industries of foreign countries. In 1897, on the recommendation of Mr. Frederic Emory, then chief of the Bureau of Foreign Commerce of the Department of State, the usefulness of the American series was greatly enhanced by the establishment of the system of publishing daily advance sheets of the monthly issues. It is obvious that this development constituted a highly important step towards making the consular service of practical value to the business interests of the country.

American diplomacy has also exerted a potent influence upon the adoption of simple and direct methods in the conduct of negotiations. Observant of the proprieties and courtesies of intercourse, but having, as John Adams once declared, "no notion of cheating anybody," American diplomatists have relied rather upon the strength of their cause, frankly and clearly argued, than upon a subtle diplomacy, for the attainment of their ends. Nor did the framework of government adopted in the United States admit of the practice of secrecy and reserve, such as characterized the diplomacy of monarchs whose tenure was for life and who were unvexed by popular electorates and representative assemblies. Hence, as it was in the beginning, so American diplomacy has in the main continued to be, a simple, direct, and open diplomacy, the example of which has had much to do with shaping the development of modern methods. Nor should we forbear to remark that while it has, by reason of the directness with which it expresses its sentiments, sometimes been disrespectfully dubbed "shirt-sleeves" diplomacy, it may confidently invite a comparison as to the propriety of its speech and conduct with the diplomacy of other nations.

In at least one instance, however, the attempt at simplicity was carried further than in the end proved to be practicable. Washington, while President, once observed that, although he was not accustomed to impede the dispatch of business "by a ceremonious attention to idle forms," it would not be prudent for a young state to dispense altogether with rules of procedure which had "originated from the wisdom of statesmen" and were "sanctioned by the common consent of nations." But Jefferson, late in his first administration, sought to abolish all social forms and precedence. The occasion of this action was the claim of Mrs. Merry, the wife of the British minister, of the right to be taken in to dinner by the

President. In order to avoid this claim, Jefferson adopted what he called the rule of pell-mell, the meaning of which was that no particular place was to be assigned to anybody, but that each was to take what was at hand; and he sought to enforce this measure not only at his own entertainments, but also on all public occasions, such as inaugurations. This innovation was hotly resented by certain members of the diplomatic corps, and gave rise to controversies which, by reason of their spicy and entertaining quality, have enjoyed a prominence out of proportion to their historical importance. Experience soon demonstrated that social equality was not always best assured by committing the determination of questions of etiquette to individual inclination and enterprise, which perchance might seek in confusion an undue exaltation. No one could have more fully exemplified simplicity in character and in bearing than did President Madison; but on entertaining the new British minister, F. J. Jackson, in 1809, he settled the question of procedure by escorting Mrs. Jackson to dinner, while Jackson took in Mrs. Madison. Nothing could better illustrate Madison's indifference to forms than his official reception of Jackson on the latter's presentation. The affair was conducted in the same manner as a private meeting between gentlemen. After Jackson was introduced, Madison asked him to have a chair, and, says Jackson, while they were talking, a negro brought them "some glasses of punch and a seed-cake."

The effect of democratic tendencies on American diplomacy is seen in the course of the government of the United States with regard to diplomatic uniform. As early as 1817 American ministers had a prescribed dress which was fixed by the mission at Ghent. This dress consisted of a blue coat, lined with white silk; a straight cape, embroidered with gold, and single-breasted; buttons plain, or, if they could be had, with the artillerist's eagle stamped upon them; cuffs embroidered in the same manner as the cape; white cashmere breeches; gold knee-buckles; white silk stockings, and gold or gilt shoe-buckles; a three-cornered chapeau bras, not so large as that used by the French nor so small as that used by the English; a black cockade with an eagle attached, and a sword. On gala-days and other occasions of extraordinary ceremony the American ministers were allowed to wear more embroidery, as well as a white ostrich-feather, not standing erect, but sewed around the brim, in their hats. A description of the costume, together with a plate, was given to the minister as a part of his instructions. At the beginning of the administration of President Jackson the prescribed uniform was changed so that it consisted of a black coat, with a gold star on each side of the collar near its termination; underclothes of black, blue, or white, at the option of the wearer; a three-cornered chapeau bras; a black cockade and eagle; and a steel-mounted sword with a white scabbard. This dress, which was supposed to correspond with the simplicity of American institutions, was recommended but not prescribed. These instructions were, however, done away with by a circular issued by William L. Marcy, as Secretary of State, on June 1, 1853, by which American ministers were desired, as far as practicable without impairing their usefulness, to appear at court "in the simple dress of an American citizen." If this could not be done without detriment to the public interest, the nearest approach to it, compatible with the requisite performance of duties, was earnestly recommended. "The simplicity of our usages and the tone of feeling among our people is," said Marcy, "much more in accordance with the example of our first and most distinguished representative at a royal court than the practice which has since prevailed. It is to be regretted that there was ever any departure in this respect from the example of Dr. Franklin." Wharton, in his *International Law Digest*, states that the dress worn by Franklin "was Quaker full dress, being court dress in the time of Charles II."; it was, at any rate, comparatively simple. The experiences of the American ministers in carrying out Marcy's instructions were varied. The greatest difficulty was encountered by Buchanan, at London, where his proposal to appear at court without some mark indicative of his rank was the subject of peremptory objection. He finally compromised upon appearing in the dress which he wore at the receptions of the President of the United States, with the addition of a very plain black-handled and black-hilted dress sword. With this addition, he declared that he never felt prouder as a citizen of his country than when he stood amid the brilliant circle of foreign ministers and other court dignitaries "in the simple dress of an American citizen." At Paris, Henry S. Sanford, who was then acting as *chargé d'affaires ad interim* of the United States, was permitted to appear at the Tuileries in citizen's dress. When, however, the new minister, John Y. Mason, arrived, he decided, after consultation with the French officials, to adopt a uniform, and had a costume devised which was described by Sanford as "a coat embroidered with gilt tinsel, a sword and cocked hat, the invention of a Dutch tailor in Paris, borrowed chiefly from the livery of a subordinate *attaché* of legation of one of the petty powers of the Continent." Sanford, conceiving Mason's conduct to involve an oblique censure of his own course, resigned his position as secretary in disgust.

At The Hague, August Belmont was permitted to appear in citizen's dress, although it was stated that his appearance in uniform "would have been better liked." At Lisbon, John L. O'Sullivan appeared at court in "an ordinary evening suit," consisting of a blue coat and black trousers, with "a simple American button" indicating his representative capacity. At Berlin it was declared that the King "would not consider an appearance before him without costume respectful"; and the American minister thereupon provided himself with a court dress which he described as "very plain and simple." At Stockholm, the King expressed his willingness to receive the representative of the United States in an audience for business in any dress his government might prescribe, but added, "In the society of my family and on occasions of court no one can be received but in court dress, in conformity with established custom." The minister therefore appeared at court in the costume which he had previously worn. By a joint resolution, approved March 27, 1867, Congress prohibited persons in the diplomatic service of the United States "from wearing any uniform or official costume not previously authorized by Congress." By Section 34 of the act of July 28, 1866, however, officers who have served in the civil war as volunteers in the armies of the United States are authorized to bear their official title, and upon occasions of ceremony to wear the uniform of the highest grade they have held, by brevet or other commissions, in the volunteer service. In spite of these statutes, diplomatic officers of the United States, while not adopting what might be called a uniform, have often worn, as Buchanan did in London, some article of apparel suggestive of their official station and rank.

INFLUENCE AND TENDENCIES

The subject of diplomatic dress has been introduced, not because it was in itself of great moment, but because it illustrates the development of that democratic spirit, often described in contemporary writings as "American feeling," which was perhaps most ebullient in the middle of the last century. Since that time great changes have taken place, and with the increased complexity of social activities, the extraordinary growth of private fortunes, and the wonderful advance of the nation as a whole in wealth and power, simplicity has become less and less a distinctive trait of the life of the Republic, either at home or abroad. On the other hand, there has grown up a visible tendency towards conformity to customs elsewhere established, and the progress of this tendency has been accelerated by the natural drift of a great and self-conscious people towards participation in what are called world-affairs.

The first joint international treaty, with reference to a question not distinctively American, to which the government of the United States became a party, was the convention concluded on October 22, 1864, jointly with Great Britain, France, and the Netherlands, in relation to the payment by Japan of the Shimonoseki indemnity. Three years later a joint convention was concluded between the same powers and Japan for the establishment of tariff duties in the latter country. By reason of a common interest, the United States was thus led in the Far East to depart from its usual policy of making only separate or independent agreements with other nations. No similar departure had then been made in China, but the policy of concerted action with other powers had already been entered upon in that country as well as in Japan—a policy which has eventuated in the allied march to Peking in 1900 and in the conclusion of the convention of September 7, 1901, between the allies and China. This convention, which embraces questions of politics as well as of commerce, is the most comprehensive joint arrangement to which the United States has ever become a signatory. The United States has, however, as a member of the great family of nations, become a party to other joint international agreements, such as the Geneva convention for the amelioration of the condition of the wounded in the field; the convention for the protection of submarine cables outside territorial waters; the Madrid convention with reference to the protégé system in Morocco; the international union for the protection of industrial property; the international postal union; and the treaties concluded at The Hague with reference to the laws and customs of war on land, the adaptation to maritime warfare of the principles of the Geneva convention, and the pacific adjustment of international disputes.

Intimacy of association, though it does not destroy the spirit of emulation, tends to produce uniformity in manners and customs. Of the operation of this rule, a striking example may be seen in the act of Congress by which provision was made for the appointment of ambassadors. Prior to the passage of this act it had been assumed to be undesirable to introduce into the American diplomatic service a grade of officials deriving extraordinary ceremonial privileges from the fact that they were supposed in a peculiar sense to represent the "person" of the "sovereign." William L. Marcy, when Secretary of State, naturally declined to recommend the creation of such a class. Secretary of State Frelinghuysen, viewing the matter in a practical light, thought it would be unjust to American ministers to increase their rank without raising their salaries, and that Congress could not with propriety be asked to make them "an allowance commensurate with the necessary mode of life of an ambassador." Mr. Bayard, who was afterwards to become the first American ambassador, declared, when Secretary of State, that "the benefits attending a higher grade of ceremonial treatment" had not "been deemed to outweigh the inconveniences which, in our simple social democracy, might attend the reception in this country of an extraordinarily foreign privileged class." Nevertheless, in 1893, the higher grade was introduced. For this measure it will scarcely be claimed that there was any necessity. In the days before American ambassadors existed, a visitor to London sought to learn who was the most important "ambassador" at the court of St. James. A European member of the diplomatic corps, to whom the inquiry was addressed, promptly responded, "The American minister." From time to time, however, American representatives abroad, wishing to enjoy the ceremonial privileges of the ambassadorial rank, recommended its creation; and eventually their recommendation was adopted. But it was done without any increase of compensation, so that to-day none but a man of fortune can afford to be an American ambassador. When we scan the list of those who have thus far held the position, it is not difficult to believe that the Republic has as yet suffered no detriment by reason of this moral limitation upon the choice of its agents; but the creation of conditions under which persons of moderate means are excluded from the highest public employments, except at a sacrifice which they can ill afford to make or cannot make at all, is not in harmony with what have been conceived to be American ideals.

To this incongruity it is within the power of Congress at any time to apply a corrective; but there is yet another innovation the remedy for which lies with the executive branch of the government. Among the extraordinary privileges commonly said to belong to the ambassador, by reason of his representing the "person" of the "sovereign," is that of personal audience on matters of business with the head of the state. In Europe, with the substitution of constitutional governments for absolute monarchies, this privilege has become merely nominal, but in Washington it has been revived in something like its pristine rigor, direct intercourse with the President, without regard to the Secretary of State, being constantly demanded and practised. In the days when the highest rank was that of envoy extraordinary and minister plenipotentiary, the privilege of transacting diplomatic business directly with the President was rarely accorded to a foreign minister, not only because the time of the President was supposed to be already sufficiently occupied, but also because the White House is not an office of record, the custodian of the diplomatic archives being the Secretary of State, who is the legal organ and adviser of the President in foreign affairs, and who, by reason of his preoccupation with the business of his own department, is supposed to possess that mastery of its details which is so essential to the care of public as well as of private interests. The President, with his multifarious duties and responsibilities, is certainly entitled to all the freedom of discretion which the rulers of other countries enjoy with regard to the direct management of diplomatic business.

But without regard to methods, which from time to time may change, there is no doubt that the importance of the United States as a factor, not in the "concert of Europe," but in that wider concert which embraces all civilized powers, Eastern as well as Western, is destined to grow. In 1871 a conference at Washington, presided over by the Secretary of State, resulted in the conclusion of a permanent truce between Spain and the allied republics on the west coast of South America, thus formally ending an unfortunate conflict in the Western Hemisphere. In 1905 the whole world rings with praise of the President of the United States, who, quick to seize the critical moment, successfully interposed for the termination of the titanic struggle between Russia and Japan in the Far East. In his triumph there was no doubt a large personal element. But it is also true that from his fortunate station he was able to speak on this occasion with an impartial and authoritative benevolence which no other ruler could invoke. The results afford a convincing proof of the nation's power; and not merely of its power, but also of the exercise of that highest influence which proceeds not so much from material forces as from the pursuit of those elevated policies that have identified American diplomacy with the cause of freedom and justice.

BIBLIOGRAPHY

ADAMS, HENRY, *History of the United States during the Administrations of Jefferson and Madison.* 9 volumes, New York, 1889–1891.

ADAMS, JOHN QUINCY, *Memoirs, Comprising Portions of His Diary from 1795 to 1848.* 12 volumes, Philadelphia, 1874–1877.

ALLEN, GARDNER W., *Our Navy and the Barbary Corsairs.* Boston and New York, 1904.

AMERICAN ACADEMY OF POLITICAL AND SOCIAL SCIENCE, *The Foreign Policy of the United States, Political and Commercial.* Philadelphia, 1899. *The United States and Latin America.* Philadelphia, 1903.

BACOURT, ADOLPHE DE, *Souvenirs d'un Diplomate: Lettres Intimes sur l'Amérique.* Paris, 1882.

BANCROFT, FREDERIC, *Life of William H. Seward.* 2 volumes, New York, 1900.

BANCROFT, GEORGE, *History of the Formation of the Constitution of the United States of America.* New York, 1885.

BARBÉ MARBOIS, FRANÇOIS, MARQUIS DE, *The History of Louisiana, particularly of the Cession of that Colony to the United States of America, with an Introductory Essay on the Constitution and Government of the United States.* Lawrence's translation, Philadelphia, 1830.

BEMIS, GEORGE, *American Neutrality: its Honorable Past, its Expedient Future.* Boston, 1866.

BERNARD, MOUNTAGUE, *A Historical Account of the Neutrality of Great Britain during the American Civil War.* London, 1870.

CHANNING and HART, *Guide to the Study of American History.* Boston, 1897.

Compilation of Reports of Committee on Foreign Relations, United States Senate, 1789–1901. Senate Executive Documents, 231, 56th Congress, 2d Session, pts. 1 to 8.

CUSHING, CALEB, *The Treaty of Washington: its Negotiation, Execution, and the Discussions relating thereto.* New York, 1873.

DONIOL, HENRI, *Histoire de la Participation de la France à l'Établissement des États-Unis d'Amérique. Correspondance Diplomatique et Documents.* 5 volumes, Paris, 1886–1892.

FOSTER, JOHN WATSON, *A Century of American Diplomacy, 1776–1876.* Boston, 1900.
—— *American Diplomacy in the Orient.* Boston, 1903.

HART, ALBERT BUSHNELL, *Hand-book of the History, Diplomacy, and Government of the United States.* Cambridge, 1901.
—— *The Foundations of American Foreign Policy.* New York, 1901.

HENDERSON, JOHN B., JR., *American Diplomatic Questions.* New York, 1901.

LATANÉ, JOHN HOLLADAY, *The Diplomatic Relations of the United States and Spanish America.* Baltimore, 1900.

LYMAN, THEODORE, *The Diplomacy of the United States, being an Account of the Foreign Relations of the Country, from the first Treaty with France in 1778.* 2d edition, 2 volumes, Boston, 1828.

MAHAN, ALFRED THAYER, *The Problem of Asia and its Effect on International Policies.* Boston, 1900.

MOORE, JOHN BASSETT, *History and Digest of the International Arbitrations to which the United States has been a*

BIBLIOGRAPHY

Party, together with Appendices Containing the Treaties Relating to Such Arbitrations, and Historical and Legal Notes on Other International Arbitrations Ancient and Modern, and on the Domestic Commissions of the United States for the Adjustment of International Claims. 6 volumes, Washington, 1898.

MOORE, JOHN BASSETT, *A Treatise on Extradition and Interstate Rendition.* 2 volumes, Boston, 1891.

—— *A Digest of International Law.* In press.

PÉTIN, HECTOR, *Les États-Unis et la Doctrine de Monroe.* Paris, 1901.

REDDAWAY, WILLIAM FIDDIAN, *The Monroe Doctrine.* Cambridge, England, 1898.

RHODES, JAMES FORD, *History of the United States from the Compromise of 1850.* 5 volumes, New York, 1893–1901.

RICHARDSON, JAMES D., compiler, *A Compilation of the Messages and Papers of the Presidents, 1789–1897.* 10 volumes, Washington, 1896–1899.

ROOSEVELT, THEODORE, *The Winning of the West, 1769–1807.* 4 volumes, New York, 1889–1896.

RUSH, RICHARD, *Memoranda of a Residence at the Court of London, 1817–1819.* Philadelphia, 1833. Second series, 1819–1825. Philadelphia, 1845. Also edited by Benjamin Rush under the title of *The Court of London, 1819–1825.* London, 1873.

SCHOULER, JAMES, *History of the United States of America under the Constitution.* Revised edition, 6 volumes, New York, 1895–1899.

SCHUYLER, EUGENE, *American Diplomacy and the Furtherance of Commerce.* New York, 1886.

SNOW, FREEMAN, *Treaties and Topics in American Diplomacy.* Boston, 1894.

TRESCOT, WILLIAM HENRY, *The Diplomacy of the Revolution: an Historical Study.* New York, 1852.

AMERICAN DIPLOMACY

TRESCOT, WILLIAM HENRY, *The Diplomatic History of the Administrations of Washington and Adams, 1789–1801.* Boston, 1857.

TUCKER, GEORGE FOX, *The Monroe Doctrine: a Concise History of its Origin and Growth.* Boston, 1885.

WHARTON, FRANCIS, *A Digest of the International Law of the United States.* 3 volumes, Washington, 1887.

WHEATON, HENRY, *History of the Law of Nations in Europe and America from the Earliest Times to 1842.* New York, 1845.

WINSOR, JUSTIN, *The Mississippi Basin: the Struggle in America between England and France, 1697–1763.* Boston, 1895.

—— *The Westward Movement: the Colonies and the Republic West of the Alleghanies, 1763–1798.* Boston, 1897.

WOOLSEY, THEODORE SALISBURY, *America's Foreign Policy: Essays and Addresses.* New York, 1898.

The collected works of American statesmen, and especially those of Washington, John Adams, Jefferson, Franklin, Hamilton, Madison, Monroe, Gallatin, Webster, Calhoun, Seward, Summer.

INDEX

271

INDEX

INDEX

Cushing, Caleb, envoy to China, 122; views on expatriation, 176; counsel at Geneva, 210, 268.

DANA, FRANCIS, mission to Russia, 15, 19.
Danish West Indies, attempts to annex, 246.
Dauphin, the, an American ship, seized by Algerine cruiser, 66.
Davis, J. C. B., American agent at Geneva, 210.
Deane, Silas, secret agent to France, 5, 6; surrender as a rebel demanded, 15; commissioner to France, 8.
Debts, confiscated, engagement to pay, 28, 29, 34.
Decatur, Commodore, dealings with Barbary powers, 70, 71.
Declaration of Independence, 2, 6, 168, 248, 250, 251.
Declaration of intention. *See* Naturalization.
Declaration of Paris, 61.
Denmark, claim to monopolize fisheries, 87; abolition of sound dues, 81, 82; question of ceding West India possessions, 246; arbitrations, 215.
"Department of foreign affairs," 5 *n*.
Dickinson, John, member of "Committee of Secret Correspondence," 6.
Diplomacy, American. *See* American diplomacy.
Diplomacy, element of chance, 25; questionable practices, 19.
Diplomatic dress, controversies concerning, 257–261.
Diplomatic life, 15.
Directory, French, refusal to receive Pinckney, 57–59.
Discriminating duties, abolition of, 12, 117–119.

Divine right, principle of, 4.
Dogger Bank incident, 220.
Dominican republic. *See* Santo Domingo.
Doniol, French and American relations, 268.
Dress, diplomatic. *See* Diplomatic dress.
"Due diligence," test of neutral duty, 50.
Dumas, C. W. F., his services to the United States, 21–25.
Dupuy de Lôme, Señor, Spanish minister, his withdrawal, 141.
Duties, discriminating. *See* Discriminating duties.

EATON, GENERAL WILLIAM, capture of Derne, 70.
Ecuador, arbitrations with, 215.
Elgin, Lord, reciprocity and fisheries treaty, 93, 94.
Elliot, Hugh, British minister at Berlin, theft of Arthur Lee's papers, 19–23.
Embargoes, 61.
Emory, Frederic, development of consular reports, 254.
Empress of China, American ship, arrival at Canton, 1784, 119.
England. *See* Great Britain.
Etiquette, diplomatic, controversies as to, 255, 257.
European powers, attitude of, towards American Revolution, 17–19.
Eustis, William, captured on the *Trent*, 74.
Evarts, William M., counsel at Geneva, 210; establishment of consular reports, 254.
Everett, A. H., empowered to negotiate with Japan, 126.
Everett, Edward, views on expatriation, 175.
Expansion, territorial, of the United States, 13, 223–247;

275

INDEX

tion, 190; arbitrations, 214, 215.

Franklin, Benjamin, member of "Committee of Secret Correspondence," 6; solicits aid of C. W. F. Dumas, 24; commissioner to France, 8; voyage to France, 15; correspondence with Shelburne, 25, 26; proposals for peace, 27; opposition to claims of loyalists, 28; position as to confiscated debts, 28; attitude towards France, 29–31; commissioned to treat with Barbary powers, 65; negotiator of treaties, 33; advocates immunity of private property at sea, 61; dress, 258.

Frederick the Great, 21.

Freedom, principle of, 2, 6.

Free port acts, 113.

"Free ships free goods," 54.

Frelinghuysen, F. T., views as to ambassadorial rank, 263.

French consuls, assumption of admiralty powers, 44, 45.

French Revolution, attitude of United States, 35, 36, 143; course of Gouverneur Morris, 37, 38.

Fur-seal arbitration. *See* Bering Sea controversy.

Gallatin, Albert, effort to abolish commercial restrictions, 113, 116.

Genêt, Edmond C., French minister to United States, 38–41, 43, 44; recall, 44, 48.

Geneva arbitration, 207, 210, 211.

Geneva convention, 262.

George III. advised to recognize American independence, 25.

Germany, acceptance of Mon-

roe Doctrine, 158, 164; Samoan policy, 240;

Gerry, Elbridge, envoy to France, 57–59.

Ghent, treaty of, stipulation against slave-trade, 78; arbitrations, 208.

Gibraltar, Strait of, navigation, 64, 65, 71, 72.

Glynn, Commander, visit to Japan, 126.

Gore, Christopher, arbitrator under Jay treaty, 204.

Government, acts of, 4.

Gram, Gregers, Bering Sea arbitrator, 213.

Grant, U. S., attitude towards Cuba, 140; attempts to annex Santo Domingo, 245.

Gray, Captain Robert, discovery of Columbia River, 234.

Great Britain, acquisition of Canada and the Island of Cape Breton, 7; maritime supremacy, 15; ubiquitous agencies for obtaining information, 19; war against the Netherlands, 17; rule of war of 1756, 59; peace of 1782, 29; treaties with, 33; retention of northern posts, 34; Jay treaty, 56; violations of neutral rights, 56, 59–61; trade with the Mediterranean, 65; trade excluded from Hanover, 60; efforts to suppress slave-trade, 76; treaty with China, 122; attitude towards Holy Alliance, 145; acceptance of Monroe Doctrine, 157, 159; law of allegiance, 178, 179, 184; naturalization treaty with United States, 188, 189; system of extradition, 252.

Greeks, struggle for independence, 136.

Grenville, Lord, negotiations with Jay, 110, 202.

INDEX

INDEX

Reprisal, frigate, 15, 16.

Revolution. *See* American Revolution; French Revolution.

Rights of man, 4, 5. *See also* Natural rights.

Rivers, free navigation, 82–85.

Roberts, Edmund, agent to Far East, 120, 121, 125; treaty with Siam, 121; with Muscat, 121.

Robinson, Christopher, counsel in fur-seal arbitration, 213.

Robinson, W. E., advocates doctrine of expatriation, 185.

Rockingham, Lord, forms British cabinet, 25, 26.

Roosevelt, Theodore, exposition of Monroe Doctrine, 157; application to Santo Domingo, 165; recognition of Panama, 144; advocates immunity of private property at sea, 62; good offices between Russia and Japan, 266; *Winning of the West*, 269.

Rule of the war of 1756, 59.

Rush, Richard, contest with commercial restrictions, 113; Monroe Doctrine, 146–148; character as diplomatist, 147; memoirs, 268.

Russborough, Lord, at Berlin, 22.

Russell, Earl, demand for release of Mason and Slidell, 74; orders for detention of the *Alabama*, 52, 53.

Russell, Sir Charles, counsel in fur-seal arbitration, 213.

Russia, attitude towards American Revolution, 19; mission of Francis Dana, 15; aspirations to become a commercial power, 55; arbitration of slave question, 208; cession of Alaska, 236; peace conference at The Hague, 219; position on expatriation, 191; peace with Japan, 266.

St. Croix River, arbitration, 202, 203.

St. Lawrence River, free navigation, 83.

St. Thomas, Island of. *See* Danish West Indies.

Salisbury, Lord, attitude as to Venezuelan boundary, 154.

Salvador, proposal of annexation, 242; arbitrations, 215.

Samana Bay, efforts to acquire, 244.

Samoa, policy towards, 239–241; general act of Berlin, 240; division of islands, 240, 241.

Sanford, Henry S., 259.

San Jacinto, the, capture of the *Trent*, 74.

San Juan water boundary, 209, 212.

Santo Domingo, recognition of, 250; attempts to annex, 244; arbitrations, 215; Monroe Doctrine, 165.

Sayre, Stephen, companion of Arthur Lee, 20, 22.

Schenck, Robert C., member of joint high commission of 1871, 210.

Schulenburg, Count, Prussian minister of foreign affairs, 20.

Schuyler, Eugene, work on American diplomacy, 268.

Sclopis, Count Frederic, arbitrator at Geneva, 210.

Seals. *See* Fur-seal arbitration.

Search, right of, 63. *See also* Visit and search.

Seas, freedom of, 63, 72–81.

Selborne, Lord, counsel at Geneva, 210. *See also* Palmer, Sir Roundell.

Seminole war, 232.

Senate, United States, amends Jay treaty, 111; opposition to visit and search, 77, 78; debates fisheries treaty in open session, 97.

INDEX

THE END